Fresh
Bread

Fresh Bread

and Other Gifts of Spiritual Nourishment

Joyce Rupp, osm

Ave Maria Press
Notre Dame, Indiana 46556

I lovingly and gratefully dedicate
this work of my heart to
Mother and Dad
who have always been "Fresh Bread" to me
and to
all my friends in Harrison County, Iowa
whose lives, love, and faith
have nourished this book.

First printing, February, 1985
Seventh printing, August, 1995
80,000 copies in print

Excerpts from THE JERUSALEM BIBLE, copyright ©1966 by Darton,
Longman & Todd, Ltd. and Doubleday & Company, Inc. Used with
permission of the publisher.

Library of Congress Catalog Card Number: 85-70020

International Standard Book Number: 0-87793-283-2

Printed and bound in the United States of America

Acknowledgments

When I think of all the people who have supported my endeavors in writing *Fresh Bread*, I realize that I could have several pages of names listed here. I am very grateful to all those who have stood by me, believed in me, and encouraged me, especially my family and my Servite community. I also thank the following people who have given significant help as I prepared the manuscript:

—my typist, Evelyn Pitt, who first encouraged me to write this book and kept reminding me to take the time to do it.

—the readers of my manuscript, who gave such excellent insights and suggestions for rewriting: Fr. Bill Fitzgerald, David and MaryJo Pederson, Ginny Silvestri, OSM, and Joy Weideman, OSM.

—Evangelista Griffin, OSM, for her many hours of proofreading the scripture references, and Paula Callahan, OSM, for her literary skills which stretch way back to my high school days when she taught me English.

—Emily Palmer, OSM, who blessed my hands when they most needed it.

—Pat Callone, for leading me to Dixie Lee Segnar who was a marvelous help in learning the skills of manuscript preparation.

—Anne and Paul Bratney, for the use of their home as a quiet place to write and reflect.

—and special thanks to my editor, Frank Cunningham. I will always remember his kindness to me and to my manuscript as he carefully edited it.

Contents

Foreword

This morning I met with a 92-year-old woman whose heart is still hungry for God, a woman in the autumn of her years who expressed a restless yearning to be filled with God's love. I listened to her, I connected inwardly with so many other people who have confirmed my belief that there is a tremendous need to nourish the spiritual dimension of our lives—this dimension which can so easily be overlooked or forgotten in our crazy, hectic, tightly scheduled, work-oriented lives.

Too often we separate our spiritual life from the rest of our life. It is so easy to put it aside for more seemingly urgent or significant aspects of our days. These external aspects seem more urgent, yet are often empty without benefit of inner refreshment and nourishment. We can so easily give in to discouragement or forget our vision and our dreams when we do not take time to integrate our outer world with our inner world. We remain fragmented instead of drawing together all the pieces into a wholeness that gives our life meaning. This integration is accomplished by taking time to look at the very ordinary parts of our day, to pray them by holding them up to the light of the scripture, to celebrate them in the depths of our being by pausing to reflect and reverence them, knowing that the God of graciousness is always there, immanently present, active, drawing us into a deeper love relationship.

I am firmly convinced that we are effective in Christian leadership only if our hearts as well as our minds have come to know the God of our lives. I believe that this "knowing God" comes about in many ways but that it can only be deeply rooted in us with the nourishment of regular personal prayer.

Six years ago when I began a ministry of adult learning and spirituality in five rural parishes, I knew that one of my main goals would be to invite people to give a portion of their day to this inner nourishment. I knew that I could not ask these busy people to come to another meeting and I knew that I could not ask them to spend long periods of time in prayer. But I could realistically ask them to give 15 minutes a day to personal prayer, using the scriptures as a foundation and a journal as a tool for integration and further reflection. I knew that this time could be *quality* time. It could be a wonderful morsel of strength and sustenance for hearts that hungered for God but did not believe that there was time, energy, or room in their daily schedule for feeding that hunger.

This is how a monthly newsletter entitled *Fresh Bread* developed. Each month I would pause to look into my own heart of hearts, to perceive what was happening there. I would identify and name what I found. Then I would integrate this "inner look" with what was happening in my "outside world": the events, circumstances, situations and relationships of my life. In trying to make connections from the inside to the outside of myself, I would ask questions as to the meaning and value of what I had named:

—What is this saying to me about who I am?

—How is it affecting my growth as a person?

—What are my values and beliefs and are they evident in what has been taking place?

—Do other people think and feel this way?

—Would it be meaningful and encouraging for others if I shared these inner connections with them?

I then chose a monthly theme for personal reflection and prayer. These themes spoke out of the ordinary moments of life and touched a common thread of people's inner seasons. I found that if I were willing to go down deeply enough into my own inner world, and identify what was there, that it would then speak deeply to other people. I discovered that as different and unique as we all are, we are very much alike when we move to the deeper levels of existence.

As I sent this newsletter each month to adult leaders, I found that this little "slice of bread" made a difference. It was just enough to help them ponder their own lives and make their own connections, to encourage them to be faithful to that daily time of inner nourishment.

My hope for you is that *Fresh Bread* . . . will provide this same kind of nourishment and feed the hungers of your spirit.

—Sister Joyce Rupp, OSM

How to Use This Book

Fresh Bread . . . is a book meant to be used regularly throughout the year. It begins with January, the first month of the calendar year, but you need not start there. Simply begin with the month that most closely follows your acquiring the book.

It asks for a commitment of a definite time each day. Begin on the first day of the month by reading and pondering the opening reflection and essay of the chapter which establishes the theme for the month. Then on the following days read and reflect on the related scripture texts that are suggested, using one text per day. Other prayers and reflections developing the theme are included in each chapter to assist in your daily prayer.

The book also encourages keeping a journal as a means of integrating life and prayer. To help with this, a question is provided for each week. Respond to the question in your journal, drawing also on the week's scripture readings and other reflections and prayers offered in the chapter. An alternate use of the questions is for discussion between spouses, family members or other faith-sharing groups.

Whether or not you keep a journal, it will be helpful to you at the end of each month to review your prayer activity for that month—either in writing or in quiet reflection.

A whole batch of bread is made holy
if the first handful of dough is made holy.
Romans 11:16

Jesus, first Bread blessed and broken, you ask me to be your leaven. You lift me to your Father and gift me with your loving.

I, just a handful of dough, am asked to be the leaven for a whole batch of people so that faith will rise in hearts. It is humbling to be your leaven. It is risky to be your holy. It is goodness to be your dough.

11

I, just a handful of dough, am called by you to be kneaded, to bear the imprints of trust, giving life shaped by daily dyings.

I, just a handful of dough, know so little about being leaven. Yet, you lift me up repeatedly, telling me that you love me, assuring me with the truth that you are my rising strength.

Jesus, first one blessed and broken, make of me a good handful of dough, one who trusts enough to be kneaded, one who loves enough to be shared.

INTRODUCTION
A Handful of Dough

One September afternoon I sat with 12 members of a parish council. I opened my hand and held out a package of dry yeast. I knew there must have been some bread bakers among the group because they smiled knowingly. I shook the package and the tiny pellets of yeast rattled crisply against each other. As I looked at the group, I said: "You are like this little package of yeast. You have so much potential as leaders in this parish. You can become a handful of dough made holy—leavened—so the rest of the parish can be holy. You are meant to be the leaven of faith for others."

I could tell by their eyes that they understood. I could also sense that they were a bit frightened and overwhelmed at the thought, so I continued: "It sounds a bit scary, I know, to think of being God's leaven for others. Yet, holiness is so simple. You are more holy than you know. You probably take for granted that you believe in Jesus, that you want to pray, that you worship his Father, that you have a heart of love and a desire to care for others. This is all a part of holiness. Being the 'handful of dough made holy' is bringing this quality of faith into everyday life and seeing God's activity in the simple and the ordinary moments of our living."

It was with this beginning that we then explored, reflected upon and prayed what being a "handful of dough" means. The following 12 chapters are based upon this understanding.

Being a "handful of dough made holy" means:
Meeting God and knowing God. It is a knowing with one's head and with one's heart. It is a knowing which comes about by taking what has been given to us intellectually about our God in the scriptures, in tradition, and in all of life and then pondering this in openness, freedom and vulnerability, taking it into our hearts and allowing it to transform us. This knowing of the other in our lives in a personal way comes about by walking through our very ordinary days, walking with a heart that is open to sur-

prises and wonders in the simple beauty of people and events. It comes about through a listening spirit, one that is sensitive to the graced insight of the moment and aware of the feelings that accompany that insightful moment. It is based on the belief that it is out of the daily stream of busy-ness and activity, "the here and now," that we often experience the revelation of God and the blessing of sacramentality.

Giving oneself to the process of reflection. Reflection is that moment, minute, or hour, in which we pause inwardly and ponder the message that lies deeper than what is being seen, heard, tasted, touched or smelled. Reflection is an attunement of the imaginative and the intuitive parts of our inner being. It is developed by *discipline*—by using regular spaces in the day to deliberately pause to think about what is before us. We come to these reflective times believing that God dwells within and that these times are meant to free us to be receptive and responsive to this loving presence.

Trusting enough to be a servant of the Lord. This trusting means that we are ready and willing to be "kneaded," to be open to the struggle and the pain that may come, to be transformed from a tiny handful of dough into a living loaf of bread. This trusting develops when we are praying daily to be present to others with the attitude of Jesus, when we are constantly aware of the great need to lean on the love and the strength of God. At those times we are stretched and are called on to let go, to let the rising happen. This trusting is lifelong and always needs to be encouraged by other trusting hearts who are "handfuls of dough."

Feeding the hunger for God that is deep within us. Nourishment of our spirit takes time and discipline. Sometimes we allow our spirit to hunger and thirst for days without offering ourselves good food for inner growth. Feeding our hunger for God means not only setting aside definite time but also using good resources such as scripture for our prayer time. The food that we place in our minds and hearts greatly affects the decisions and the choices of our days.

Giving of ourselves to others with quality presence. Quality presence means we have a heart of love and a desire to care for others. It means that "being with" is just as significant as "doing for." It means being willing to have nothing to show for our day's work except faithfully standing by the cross of another, or giving love in a celebrative moment, or attentive perceptive listening with our heart. This kind of presence creates peace, energy, and acceptance in the heart of another. Quality moments mean forgetting about clocks and calendars.

Wanting to be holy, wanting to be a saint. Holiness is knowing we have tasted God and knowing that we can never be satisfied with just that taste. It is choosing, in spite of our fear, to go more deeply. Holiness is facing the pain of the world and crying out with its suffering. Holiness is stopping to gasp in amazement at how love stirs in the joy and beauty of ordinary events. Holiness is feeling an awesome restlessness that pursues us even though we try to run away from it. Holiness is choosing to keep on struggling and believing that there is such a thing as eternal life, that there is such a one as eternal love. Holiness is wanting to be a saint. It is knowing God as a companion on the journey of life.

Believing in one's potential to be the handful of dough. Yes, we are the "handfuls of dough made holy so that the whole batch of bread can be made holy."

Each time you eat bread, take a moment to pray for those entrusted to your care; remember how you are meant to be the handful of dough, the leaven of faith, for others. Use the cover from a package of yeast as a bookmark in your bible, to remind you of your call to be holy. Decide on a regular time each day when you will deliberately pause for prayer, reading, and keeping a journal. Allow that time to be leaven for you so that all of your life will be transformed in God. Thus you will become a blessing for many.

can it be?
have I for so long
forgotten to feed myself?

yes.
for nigh a year now
I was slowly starving.
getting lost in busy days,
tossing aside the hunger
that chewed away inside.

yet, I did not die.
by some quiet miracle
I made it to this moment
of truth:

I nearly starved to death.

it was not my body
that I failed to feed.
it was my spirit,
left alone for days
without nourishment or care.

and then one day
I paused to look within,
shocked at what I found:
so thin of faith,
so weak of understanding,
so needy of encouragement.

my starving spirit cried the truth:

I can!
I will!
I must
be fed!

♣ JANUARY:

A New Snowfall

Freshness

a new year is moving in
just as surely as the winter
walks along in snowflakes

and I sit here wondering
in the breath of his bless
and the glance of his grace

I think about the year now gone
and how I've walked across it
(it grieves me some and joys me some)

and as the new year stretches
I wonder how I'll meet it
will I let his grace find me
and will I let him charm me
and will I let his truth possess me
and will I let him lead me
and will I take his love to heart
and fix my gaze on him

oh how I wonder with this heart of mine
so often gone astray
so often found in desert
so often hid in hills of wind and wild

I wonder how I'll meet this year
and if I'll give myself the chance
to catch the breath of bless
and glance of his dear grace
to rise and walk from sinfulness
to come return and find him waiting
to reach and know that he can heal
to turn around and give up all
and let him be my treasure

a new year is moving in
just as surely as the winter
walks along in snowflakes

my God is moving in again
and just like winter snow
he breathes my life full freshness

It was the first day of the new year. I awoke that morning to a magnificent wonderland: sun sparkling on a fresh snowfall, tree limbs lined a white loveliness. The snow had transformed the earth from the drabness of a barren landscape. As I rejoiced in this beauty, I remembered a line from Gerard Manley Hopkins: "There lies the dearest freshness deep down things." Looking at the pure touch of snow I felt that "dearest freshness" resting on the land and also resting deeply inside of me. It was the new year. It was the time to ponder the past and make marks for the future. The "freshness" held my attention and drew me into prayerful reflection. "Yes," I thought. "Freshness. That's it. That is what this new year is offering me as I pray to the God of my life this sparkling morning. God is holding out a freshness of life to me. God is offering me a new beginning with this new year."

I am not so certain that we always enter into the new year with our focus on the whiteness, the freshness, the brand-new beginnings in our heart. I tend to believe that we let our glance rest a little too long on all those areas of our lives where we feel we have failed or not given our best. Why else would we still make resolutions based on what has gone before? We look into the past year and feel guilty or discouraged when we realize that we are still struggling with our failures and our weaknesses, those age-old shadows that we seem to overcome, only to discover that they still pursue us relentlessly deep inside.

It can be beneficial to glance backward over the past year if we do not stay there and center on our incompleteness. As long as we do not base all our vision of the new year on that backward glance, we can learn from what we see. But then we must move on. January is such a good time to deliberately set our steps forward, to begin again, to give ourselves over to the promises of the future. January is the month when we look, really look, at our life's journey and rejoice over the gift of another year given to us. The perception of life that enables us to walk into a new year with this hope and confidence is the perception that we can begin anew, that we are constantly being offered fresh beginnings by our God.

Close your eyes and just imagine the clean, white fluffy snow softly falling, covering all the drab spots of deadness on the earth. See that same soft, clean whiteness fall into your heart. Feel it heal the wounds, making clean your dreams and your hopes. Hear the God of new beginnings speak to you about the fresh start being offered.

It is this "God of freshness" who encourages our journey. If we are to walk into the new year hopefully, we need to look at God as well as at ourselves. When we look to the scriptures, we learn how much God desires new beginnings for us. This is a constant theme that runs through the sacred word. We hear again and again that God refreshes, renews, heals, blesses, makes whole, cleanses what has become mired, clears what has become blurred, restores what has died, recovers what has gone astray. Yahweh speaks in Isaiah and tells us that there is "no need to recall the past. . . . I am doing a new deed. . . . Now I am revealing new things to you . . . for past troubles will be forgotten and hidden from my eyes" (Is 43:18-19, 48:6, 65:17). At the beginning of the new year, we can hear Yahweh saying not only in Isaiah but in our own lives as well:

"Come now, let us talk this over. . . .
Though your sins are like scarlet,
they shall be white as snow;
though they are red as crimson,
they shall be like wool" (Is 1:18).

Jesus, too, spoke of this God, this Father of his, who heals, consoles, forgives, and encourages us to begin again. Jesus presents this Father as a deeply loving one who always gives his people another chance, God who understands the human heart, who picks us up and dusts us off when we fall into the ashes of our weaknesses. This God's love is everlasting. He encourages us by holding out a new year like an unmarred, snow-covered land, saying: "Look, it's new. It's clean. It's fresh. Let's walk it

together. Do not keep looking back. You cannot undo
the past, but you can walk the present with me. Treasure
my love for you and believe in my presence with you. I
have so many wonderful surprises if you will but begin
anew on the journey and rely on me instead of just on
yourself."

I believe that this is what our God speaks to us. This
is God's "Happy New Year" to us. Instead of simply
working hard all by ourselves on some resolutions that we
hope will change us into better people, we ought to come
before our winter God and offer ourselves to him, believing in his mercy, healing, and refreshment, trusting that
his touch is what we most need, and that this touch is a
pure, free gift. We do need to take action in our lives and
to try to break old habits and attitudes that keep us from
gospel living but we cannot force this to happen; indeed,
it cannot happen without the grace of God active in our
hearts. Just as the waiting, brown earth cannot force the
snow to fall so, too, we cannot force the inner change
we so long for. We can only be open, ready, waiting,
yearning, and believing that God yearns the same for us
and will grace our needy lives if we are receptive to the
gift being offered to us.

I invite you this month to pray the message of freshness. Think about how we end one journey and begin
another with a clean start. Pray to open up to God's everlasting love for you. Along with praying a passage of
scripture each day, I invite you to enter into some re-
minders of the freshness of God's love in your daily life.
This January you might wish to do some of the following
to increase your awareness of the freshness which God
holds out to you:

> Use imagery to connect you to freshness and to
> God's gift of new beginnings. For me, God's love is
> refreshing . . .
>
> > as taking an early morning walk
> > as catching a snowflake on my cheek
> > as taking a shower after a tennis match
> > as feeling the touch of a newly born babe

as hearing the trees filled with wrens
as smelling freshly baked bread
as drinking good, red wine

How is God's love refreshing for you?

When you go outdoors, pause to take a deep breath of fresh winter air; it can be a prayer without words, recalling the winter God's fresh love.

Make a deliberate effort to give someone a fresh start in relating to you; give someone another chance—maybe a family member, or a friend, or neighbor, or someone you work with, maybe even your own self when you are discouraged or too hard on self; maybe it means a letter to someone you have been upset with for a long time.

Pause over ordinary things like clean wash, new snowfalls, freshly baked goods, faces of children full of wonder, new shoots on plants. . . .

Remember, you are to be "*fresh* bread." May the freshness of God's lasting love for you give you a brand new start this year.

Scripture Texts for Daily Prayer

Is 42:5-9   "Fresh things I now foretell."

Is 43:16-21   "No need to recall the past. . . . See, I am doing a new deed."

Is 48:6-16   "Now I am revealing new things to you . . . created just now, this very moment."

Is 55:10-13   Freshness of rain and snow on the earth is compared to the new life of God's world.

Is 65:16-25   ". . . for past troubles will be forgotten and hidden from my eyes."

Lam 3:19-24   "The favors of Yahweh are not all past . . . every morning they are renewed."

Sir 43:13-33   "He sprinkles snow like birds alighting. . . . The eye marvels at the beauty of its whiteness."

Ez 36:15-28   "I shall pour clean water over you and you shall be cleansed. . . . I shall put my spirit in you."

Is 1:16-18   "Though your sins are like scarlet, they shall be white as snow."

Ps 4:   "You have given more joy to my heart than others ever knew."

Ps 33   "Yahweh, let your love rest on us as our hope."

Ps 46   "There is a river whose streams refresh the city of God."

Ps 51   "Put into me a new and constant spirit."

Ps 94   "In the middle of all my troubles you console me and make me happy."

Ps 104   "You give breath, fresh life begins, you keep renewing the world."

Ps 118   "Yahweh is God, he smiles on us."

Ps 121   "Yahweh . . . guards you leaving, coming back."

Ps 136   "His love is everlasting."

Ps 145	"Patiently all creatures look to you to feed them throughout the year."
Mk 2:1-12	Jesus gives a new beginning to the paralytic.
Mk 2:18-22	Jesus talks about the need to receive his message in "fresh skins."
Mk 6:30-44	Jesus saw that the people needed new energy.
Mk 7:31-37	Jesus opens up a fresh new world of sounds to a man long kept from that.
Mk 9:2-8	The privilege of seeing Jesus in a startling new way.
Jn 4:43-54	A deep faith in the new life Jesus promised.
Jn 5:19-30	Jesus speaks of the freshness of the Father who is "the source of life."
Jn 6:53-58	Jesus tells us that we will draw new life if we believe and partake in the Bread of life.
Jn 17:21-26	Jesus asks his Father to refresh us: "so that the love with which you loved me may be in them."
Heb 8:8-12	"See the days are coming . . . I will establish a new covenant. . . ."
Rev 21:1-8	"Now I am making the whole of creation new."

Welcoming a New Year

a new year stands on my doorstep
ready to enter my life's journey.

something in me welcomes this visitor:
the hope of bountiful blessings
the joy of a new beginning
the freshness of unclaimed surprises

something in me rebuffs this visitor:
the swiftness of the coming
the boldness of the entrance
the challenge of a year's good-bye

something in me fears this visitor:
the unnamed events of future days
the wisdom needed to walk love well
the demands of giving away and growing

a new year stands on my doorstep.
with fragile caution I move
to open the door for its entrance.
my heart leaps with surprise,
joy jumps in my eyes,
for there beside this brand-new year
stands my God with outstretched hand!
He smiles and gently asks of me:
can we walk this year together?

and I, so overwhelmed with goodness,
can barely whisper my reply:

welcome in!

Prayer for a New Year

O God of this new year that stretches before me,
"teach me the secrets of wisdom.
Purify me with hyssop until I am clean;
wash me until I am whiter than snow."

O God of this new year that beckons to me,
"create a clean heart in me,
put into me a new and constant spirit."

O God of this new year that holds out hope to me,
"be my savior again, renew my joy,
keep my spirit steady and willing."

O God of this new year that gives me another chance,
"in your great tenderness wipe away my faults;
wash me clean of my guilt
purify me from my sin,
For I am well aware of my faults."
Instill some joy and gladness into me.

Psalm 51:6-7, 10, 12, 1-3

Loving God, it is time to turn again to you. It is time to realize anew that I am not totally self-reliant. This is a moment full of grace that invites me to lift up my spirit to you, the one who gives freshness, the one who moves across my heart like a new snowfall and erases all the drab, brown memories of a year gone by.

Come to meet me, God of life, reach into the mystery of my self. Take me into the heart of this year and give me the confidence to journey freely, lovingly, with risk, wonder and laughter. Amen.

Questions for Journal Keeping

Week 1 "I think about the year now gone and how I've walked across it (it grieves me some and joys me some)" What grieves you about your past year? What "joys" you about your past year?

Week 2 What refreshing things do you yearn and hope for in this new year? (for self, for family or community, for work, for society, for . . .)

Week 3 When were the moments this week (or this day) when you felt a sense of God's presence blessing you with freedom?

Week 4 If you could name the most refreshing time of your life, what would it be? How did you feel and what caused this feeling? As you look over this past month, what were your most refreshing moments spiritually?

The Courageous Heart

Though I pass through a gloomy valley,
   I fear no harm;
beside me your rod and your staff
   are there, to hearten me.

                          Psalm 23:4

in the midst of quiet hills
steepled with green pines,
I heard within my heart the call
of the gentle Jesus-Shepherd.

   a haunting of my heart
   yet with consolation offered,
   for the valley indeed was dark
   and I, in need of courage.

I saw him standing there,
hand outstretched in welcome:
"Ah, little lamb, I love you.
trust in me to care well for you."

   I looked from the window
   cautious like a Much-Afraid;
   then quietly Courage knelt inside me
   and my valley of fear began to fade.

The sun took over the shadows,
the Shepherd took over my life.
I knew how precious the tenderness
and believed once more God's love.

February is the month of "the feast of hearts," Valentine's day. It is a month in which many "I love you's" are heard and sent and many little red hearts appear everywhere. All the messages and symbols of love lead me to consider one of its aspects—the courageous heart.

The winter with its harsh cold winds and layers of frozen earth leads me to reflect on courage as a wonderful gift of the human spirit. I marvel at how brave the trees and living things must be to stand so well through the wintertime. I marvel, too, at people who have come into my life in recent months, people who have that same kind of stamina, people with courageous hearts, people who have the confidence to face the winter of their lives. Jim Wolff says it well in his book *As I Have Loved You:*

> Until put to the test, no one can really know
> who or what he or she is; life alone manifests
> the quality of individual human existence.

It is not until we have faced some winters in our lives, some challenges and struggles, that we are able to know our own courage and are able to understand just how brave we can be when it is necessary to have a courageous heart.

I've discovered this courage in young parents who have chosen to care at home for their severely retarded child. I've known this courage in a middle-aged couple whose home is always open to their children who have chosen values very different from their own. I've sensed this courage in a woman who has cancer and who always has a smile and word of joy for her visitors, never indulging in self-pity or despair. I've been inspired by this courage in people who risked rejection to tell of their personal belief in Jesus, who have shared their history of weakness and pained moments.

Courage does not mean just gritting our teeth for an endurance test. Courage does mean drawing from an inner source, relying on the Lord's strength to give us the confidence we need. Courage means never giving up. It means believing that we can make it, not on our own power (although we do have a great inner resource of resiliency), but on the divine power that is always available if we ask for it. Courage is never learned overnight. It results from long years of practice and patience, being brave enough to face what life sends us. Courage is growing through the hardships of life without bitterness, discontent or disillusionment. With courage, the struggle can develop in us a mellowness and a deeper sensitivity to just how tender and special the human spirit really is.

The winter of our lives gives us the opportunity to grow in courage. The winter of our lives takes patience, self-sacrifice, self-discipline, and faithful love. Courage helps us to accept what cannot be changed and to struggle through what needs to be changed. Courage helps us to gently say what we believe, to hold on to what we know is of value despite the risk of rejection, doubt or failure. Courage enables us to offer forgiveness knowing there may be no response, to give generously of our time and have little left to warm our own weary hearts. Courage empowers us to try again when there seems to be only repeated failure, to love wholeheartedly even though all the odds seem against that love being received or returned.

This kind of courage is especially found in confident people, those who have confidence in their inner resources and in the power of God working through them. People who have the gift of courage are those who can feel angry, hurt, or depressed, yet can bounce back into life and add a bit of laughter and enthusiasm to other lives as well as their own. As I have reflected on courageous hearts, I have found some common features of confident people:

—They are willing to recognize and live with their own unfinishedness, knowing that they are subject to weakness and sometimes failures but that the best of them is good, so very good. They know they have limitations but they also know that they can rejoice in the promise of redemption.

—Despite their fears, they constantly stretch their inner selves to take risks, to meet challenges. They believe in their giftedness and know that the best way to thank God for it is to continually reach into risk, discovering and developing their hidden potential.

—They know how to laugh and to enjoy life even in the most difficult of times; they do not take themselves so seriously as to grimace and fret through each day.

—They take time for solitude—to think and to pray in order to distance themselves and get a good perspective on their present situation.

—They have their values in proper order, recognizing that people are always more important than material things, knowing that it is only the immaterial values such as love that they will carry with them into the eternal life.

—They nurture an intimate relationship with their God for they have learned that the more they know this wonderful God, the more they will understand how deeply he cherishes them no matter what happens in their lives.

—Finally, they have a vision within themselves that reminds them that their strength and power, their hope and trust, can never be mustered up all by themselves. Rather, it is God in whom they find their strength and often this God gives the needed strength through the encouragement and kindness of other human beings.

There's a beautiful dialogue in Belva Plain's novel, *Evergreen,* that speaks of human beings encouraging one another, of helping one another to continue on in adversity, to be confident that we will overcome our trials and difficulties. Part of the conversation is this:

"Human beings have so much courage.
I marvel at how much."
"I've used up all my courage."
"You'll find it again. And thank God for
giving it back to you."

This month of February, look into your own life. See where you need courage and know that you can recover it when you seem to have so little. Find it through some solitude; find it by reading the scriptures. Find it by looking into the lives of courageous folks around you. Encourage them in their own winter time with a note or a call.

Ask God to tell you about all the courage and resiliency you have hidden deep within your being. I know that the God of winter will reveal it to you and will help you to grow strong in the broken places of your lives.

Scripture Texts for Daily Prayer

Dt 31:1-8	"Be strong, stand firm . . . for Yahweh, your God is going with you."
Ps 27	"Put your hope in Yahweh, be strong, let your heart be bold. . . ."
Acts 27:21-44	"So take courage, friends; I trust in God that things will turn out just as I was told."
Lk 22:31-34	"I have prayed for you, Simon, that your faith may not fail, and once you have recovered, you in your turn must strengthen your brothers."
Phil 4:10-20	"There is nothing I cannot master with the help of the One who gives me strength."
Acts 2:1-13	New courage from the Spirit.
Acts 14:19-28	"They put fresh heart into the disciples, encouraging them. . . ."
Acts 19:8-20	". . . he spoke out boldly and argued persuasively about the kingdom of God."
Acts 23:1-11	"Next night, the Lord appeared to him and said, 'Courage!' "
Eph 3:14-21	"Glory be to him whose power, working in us, can do infinitely more than we can ask or imagine."
Phil 3:7-16	"I believe that nothing can happen that will outweigh the supreme advantage of knowing Christ Jesus my Lord."
Rom 12:3-13	"Do not give up if trials come; and keep on praying."
Col 1:24-29	". . . helped only by his power driving me irresistibly."
Rom 8:31-39	"With God on our side who can be against us?"
Lk 12:22-32	"There is no need to be afraid, little flock. . . ."
Jn 14:1-7	"Do not let your hearts be troubled."

Lk 12:4-12	"When the time comes, the Holy Spirit will teach you what you must say."
Mk 10:46-52	" 'Courage,' they said 'get up; he is calling you.' "
Dt 1:19-33	"Do not be afraid or discouraged."
Jos 1:1-9	"Be strong and stand firm. . . . Be fearless then, be confident. . . ."
Dt 8:7-20	"Remember Yahweh your God; it was he who gave you this strength. . . ."
Jn 16:31-33	"In the world you will have trouble, but be brave, I have conquered the world."
2 Cor 1:1-11	The courage gained from others.
Is 35:1-10	". . . and say to all faint hearts, 'Courage! Do not be afraid.' "
Is 40:27-31	"He gives strength to the wearied, he strengthens the powerless. . . ."
Heb 3:7-19	". . . keep encouraging one another."
Heb 10:32-36	"You will need endurance to do God's will and gain what he has promised."
Heb 12:1-13	"Think of the way he stood such opposition from sinners and then you will not give up for want of courage."
Ps 107	"Their courage was running low."

in praise of the heart of Jesus

the heart of Jesus
nearest to the Father's heart
a wellspring full of love
richness for my poverty
wholeness for my brokenness
home for my wandering
fullness for my emptiness
loving care for my selfishness
healing for my hurts
faith for my mediocrity
courage for my fears

the heart of Jesus
nearest to the Father's heart
drawing all of me to him
reaching from his heart to mine,
tender, compassionate, true,
wanting one thing only:

my loving response.

Prayer: Psalm for a Winter Day

Lord God, creator of all seasons and ages, I praise you for all that is beautiful in this winter day of February coldness: the strong, black patterns of trees standing tall, utter whiteness of snow as it layers the lawn, stillness broken only by the sound of the furnace and maybe a brave cheep of a snowbird, blue sky with morning pink still on its cheek, the bush under the rainspout drenched in ice.

Oh, all that is glistening with cold this morning, praise the Lord! All creatures snuggled away in nests, caves, trees, praise the Lord! Oh, all peoples bundled in winter wear, scurrying to work, praise the Lord! Cars, trucks, and buses chugging along the freeway, praise the Lord! Snowbirds all afluff with thick winter warmth, praise the Lord! Cows, steers, and sheep on hillsides, braving cold, praise the Lord! Oh, crunch and crackle of shoes on frosty snowfall, praise the Lord! All ponds and lakes deeply frozen and lovely formed, praise the Lord! Little rabbits leaving deep footprints 'neath my window, praise the Lord!

Yes, all the winter world, whose beauty we so often miss, whose weather we so often condemn, praise the Lord, and bless his holy name, for our world has wonders and tiny miracles if only our hearts as well as our eyes are open to see.

Questions for Journal Keeping

Week 1   What are the difficult or painful aspects of your life that beg for your courage and your confidence?

Week 2   At what moments in your life have you known the power of God working through you? When have you dipped deeply inside and relied on your inner resiliency to bounce you back into life?

Week 3   Draw a heart. In it write the names of the courageous people you know. Pray for these people each day of the coming week.

Week 4   What have you learned about the God of courage this month? What have you learned about your own heart and its courage this month? Write your prayer about courage to the winter God.

♣ MARCH

The Hidden Treasure

Lost and Found

Lord, sometimes I think your heart
is one big room of lost and found,
holding dear the timeless treasures
that I've lost through selfishness.

let me look into your heart, Lord.

is my care for hurting ones there?
(I gave it away to concerns of my own)
is my thanks for life and beauty there?
(I lost it between some busy days)

let me look deeper into your heart, Lord.

is the faith I felt so keenly there?
(I misplaced it one untrusting day)
is my willingness to be open there?
(I hid it too long and now can't find it)

is some of the truth of my self there?
(I stopped looking for it some time ago)
is my deep hunger for you waiting there?
(I lost it for food of material things)

Lord, you hold all that I value most,
it's there in the depths of your heart.
please look into your lost and found;
help me find the best of what I've lost,
to discover the values I've misplaced
and some of the treasures I've tossed away.

Have you ever experienced losing something you treasured? You never notice it's missing until the moment comes to use it, wear it, display it or pass it on to someone else. Then comes the frustration of: Did I put it somewhere for safekeeping? Did I loan it to someone? Did I carelessly discard it? Was it, perhaps, taken from me?

When we were children we played "Hide and Seek," deliberately hiding ourselves from others and waiting for them to find us in our secret hiding places. As adults we may still be playing "Hide and Seek," only now we play it with the values and treasures of our lives, hiding or losing them in the tumble of our days.

It is so easy to lose what we value. We may deeply believe in the necessity for solitude and reflection but gradually there's no space left in our day. We become so used to not having any space for solitude that finally we no longer notice that it is missing. Or we may truly believe in the need to forgive and to be reconciled, to start anew in relationships that have sharp edges or dull pain, but we allow little, hard spots in our hearts to build up into a wall that forgiveness cannot penetrate. Eventually we end up losing that warm spot in our heart for a person we once loved. We can so simply let the days and months go by without ever searching for our lost pearls of great price.

The church is wise in offering us the season of Lent because it can be the very time we need to find what is missing in our lives; it can be the season to deliberately seek what has been tossed away or misplaced or ignored, so that our lives can once again reflect the gospel which Jesus encouraged us to live. Lent can be a searching out and a restoration time and the means for renewed direction and perspective.

If we look closely into our hearts we will find that we have all lost something we value. We may have lost our patience or our integrity; we may have lost our tempers or our respect for self or for others; we may have lost hope or our capacity to understand or accept; maybe we lost a friend or perhaps our desire to pray.

Sometimes we are not even sure what we have lost, but something tells us we need to look. Something unnamed gnaws at our insides and begs us to hunt, to pursue it. It may be a giant restlessness, or a feeling of not being at home with ourselves, or an inner ache that won't go away. Perhaps it is a loss of our inner sense of direction, or a feeling that we are not sure if we have strayed from the gospel path of our beliefs and dreams.

Lent is the season to ask: What do I cherish in my life? What is it that I hide from? Am I aware of what I am missing or have misplaced interiorly? Have I given myself to the searching and finding of these treasures? What do I need to form my life more on the pattern of the Lord's death and resurrection? Who is it that I seek? Who is it that I hide from? How can I recover what I hold dear?

The gospel is filled with images of lost treasures being found. There's the lost son who returns to the arms of a father long waiting for him. There's the shepherd who searches for and who gathers into his arms the lost lamb. And there's the woman who was overjoyed at finding a precious treasure hidden in a field.

Many people in the gospel searched for something dear to them: The blind sought their sight, the woman who bled for 12 years reached out to find her health, the mute yearned to have their speech restored, the woman at the well struggled for her lost integrity, Zacchaeus discovered how much he owed the Lord, the woman who wiped the feet of Jesus found a wonderful depth of forgiveness. Jesus helped all these and more to recover what was missing in their lives.

The lost things of the gospel are treasures worth seeking. We can discipline ourselves to pray and bring those lost treasures back home to our hearts. But it takes persistence. It takes a yearning for the God of light to give direction. It takes our openness and our love of the truth.

The beauty of the finding is that all of the greatest treasures are in the heart of our God. Lent is a time to look at the Son, Jesus, and to see what he held dear, to recognize anew how he refound all of us through his death and resurrection.

Lent is a time to come to know the one who continually searches us out and finds us. Slowly read through the suggested passages of Luke's gospel. Look at Jesus, how he lived, what he calls us to be and to do, what he promises to those who are lost, and how often he found his own direction in the light of the loving Father.

Other possible ways to recover the treasures of your faith are to listen to the song "Take All the Lost Home" by Joe Wise (on the album of the same name) or to the song "Like a Shepherd" by Bob Dufford, S.J., on the album *Dwelling Place*. Be the lost one of the song; feel the shepherd find you. Know what it is like to be found by one who loves you deeply, faithfully, everlastingly.

Decide on some discipline to find your lost treasures. You may choose to fast from some food or drink in order to recover an awareness of your hunger and thirst for the Lord, or to take time with your family to rediscover the beauty of who they are. You may decide to take some time for extra prayer and spiritual reading to seek the treasure of God or you may give yourself over to the risk and vulnerability of restoring a broken relationship with someone in your life.

If there is something lost and unnamed in you, meet with someone who is wise and talk about the ache and the restlessness in your spirit.

Recover the great gospel value of caring for others by not buying something you want—give the money to the poor and the hungry instead. Write or call an aged, a lonely or a handicapped person. Give your time to someone who needs you.

As you walk through these six weeks of Lent, may you be the one who hunts in great earnest for the treasure hidden in the field of your own heart. May this Lenten season be a time when you refind those spiritual values which are so essential in shaping one's life on the pattern of the Lord Jesus.

Scripture Texts For Daily Prayer

Lk 2:22-35	A prayerful man finds the one for whom he has long been waiting.
Lk 3:1-18	The word of God finds John.
Lk 3:1-18	Jesus seeks strength in the Spirit
Lk 4:16-30	The truth of Jesus' mission is revealed in Isaiah.
Lk 4:31-37	A man possessed recovers his dignity.
Lk 4:42-44	Jesus finds inner renewal in a "lonely place."
Lk 5:1-11	Faith is found through a catch of fish.
Lk 6:20-26	The values of the gospel are found in the beatitudes.
Lk 6:27-38	Finding the treasure of true forgiveness is a gospel goal.
Lk 6:46-49	Have we lost our faith foundation?
Lk 7:1-10	Jesus finds great faith in a centurion's heart.
Lk 7:18-30	"Happy is the man who does not lose faith in me."
Lk 7:36-50	A woman finds the peace she has lost.
Lk 8:22-25	The disciples lost their faith in the power of the Lord.
Lk 9:10-17	The crowd finds Jesus and he gifts them with nourishment.
Lk 9:18-21	Peter finds the truth inside of himself.
Lk 9:28-36	The disciples discover the glory of God shining on the face of Jesus.
Lk 9:44-45	The meaning of the passion is still hidden from the disciples.
Lk 10:25-37	An example of love is found and proclaimed.
Lk 10:38-42	Mary has found "the better part."
Lk 11:5-13	Persistence in the finding: "The one who searches always finds."
Lk 11:33-36	Look for the lost light in you and let it shine.

Lk 12:22-32   Recover your trust in God; set your hearts on his kingdom.

Lk 12:33-34   Find your treasure, for "where your treasure is, there will your heart be also."

Lk 14:7-14   Have the gifts of humility, generosity, been lost?

Lk 15:4-7   "Rejoice with me . . . I have found my sheep that was lost."

Lk 15:9-10   There is rejoicing over a lost one who is found.

Lk 15:11-32   "This son of mine . . . he was lost and is found."

Lk 16:14-15   God sees what needs finding in our hearts.

Lk 19:1-10   "The Son of Man has come to seek out and save what was lost."

Lk 19:41-44   Jesus weeps over all that Jerusalem has lost.

The last week of Lent: Take the Passion narrative, chapters 22-24 of Luke. Read slowly, carefully and pray sections of this each day. Be open to finding the truth of the Paschal Mystery for you during the Holy Week.

Treasures That May Need Finding

- Have I lost a sense of purpose in life? Do I have a goal? What are my dreams and my hopes?

- Have I lost a belief in myself and my inner goodness? Do I truly care for both my body and my spirit, for the "whole" of me?

- Have I lost a generous heart? Do I give grudgingly, or only to a few, chosen ones?

- Have I lost a sensitivity to God's presence in my life? Do I run through the days without pause for reflection and remembrance?

- Have I lost the treasure of compassion? How open is my heart to the cares of others? How deeply do I feel with the pain of the world?

- Have I lost my perception of the truth? Do little lies creep into my life and does hypocrisy pursue me?

- Have I lost the gift of love? How does my life look when placed alongside the love of me in the gospels?

- Does my spirit allow for the gift of laughter? Have I lost the ability to laugh occasionally at myself and at life?

- Have I lost my vision of the Paschal mystery? What do I do with the suffering in my life? Have I forgotten how good it is to lean on the Lord?

- Have I lost my intimacy with God? Do I still know Jesus? How comfortable am I with the God of my life?

- Have I lost my heart's faithfulness to the beloved? How do I show my fidelity to those I live with (spouse, children, community . . .)?

The Lost Lamb

so much in me gets lost, God.
I run off in other directions
and lose my vision of you,
of you and of your Kingdom.

I lose sight of my hopes,
I forget all your promises.
I get lost in problems,
run around in selfishness.

there you are, before me,
waiting. calling.
there you are, behind me,
following. pursuing.
there you are, beside me,
caring, loving.

what is it you've placed
in this sheep's heart of mine?
what is it that keeps me bonded to you
in spite of all my arrogance,
in spite of all my independence?

I feel a new surge today,
a re-visioning of hope.
I feel as if you've lifted me up
and are carrying me home,
safe and secure on your shoulders,
or maybe next to your heart.

O God of lost sheep, my God,
appeal again and again
to all the lost-ness in me.
pursue me relentlessly.
carry me home. O, carry me home.

Prayer

Dear God, please find for me the things I've lost. Find for me a heart of hope and of trust. Find a love that runs silent and strong through dark days as well as bright. Find a ribbon of truth to tie around each fragment of my life. Find a joy and a peace that I can give to every hurting one. And please, Lord, find for me a faith that's big enough, mellow enough, to admit my wrongs and to trust that you will still find me and welcome me home.

O God who lifts little lost lambs close to your heart, O God who gives the heart a desire to return to you, I ask your mercy and your forgiveness for all the treasures I've misplaced. I give you thanks and praise for the beauty of finding them again. Amen.

Questions for Journal Keeping

Week 1 Read the list of "Treasures That May Need Finding." Which one most speaks to your life? Reflect on this treasure. Where and how did you lose it? How will you regain it?

Week 2 Imagine yourself to be the one of the hundred sheep who is lost. See the shepherd seek you out, embrace you, carry you home (cf. Lenten suggestions). Write your prayer to the one who has found you.

Week 3 Are there games of "Hide and Seek" that you play with your God or with others? If so, name these.

Week 4 Who have been the "shepherds" in your life who have found you? Who have been the shepherds who have brought you home to yourself or to your God? List these shepherds. Reflect on their qualities of heart.

⚓ APRIL

The Little Easters

I Have Been Entombed

I have been entombed
within the ego and the self;
I have been dead
within the walls of winter.

I have long lain aside
the hope that once I knew;
many forgotten truths
line the path of wilderness.

I have grown weary
with the waiting cocoon;
I have sensed with sorrow
the pain of transformation.

Yet, in the graceful stillness
of this early April morning,
I am greeted in love
with inside eastering.

I stand before this moment
with silent, rising sun
and page-full of Scripture
and I proclaim: *I am coming forth*!

I've left the linens of winter
lying there behind me;
I've shook off the dust of dead
and I'm bounding forth in Spirit.

It is time to break loose.
It is time to come forth.
It is time to allow life
to wing its way into depths.

This is the season of my Savior,
the One whom God raised from the dead.
This is the moment of resurrection
and I know it is the right time.

For I am coming forth,
coming forth from the tomb—
and just like my God risen,
I feel bonded with the world,
I feel all brokenness brought unto one.

I'm on my way to bless bread
with each of my dear friends;
I'm on my way to offer presence
to all those I meet on the road;
I'm on my way to bring resurrection
to all who need God's healing Life.

It is Easter
and I proclaim:
I've been raised from the dead!
I am coming forth from the tomb!

Each church year, as we celebrate that jubilant event of the Lord's resurrection, we are urged to sing "alleluias" and songs of joy. I have often wondered just how many people do feel that joy deep inside themselves. I wonder because I sometimes have a difficult time entering into the "alleluia" and I know others who also have expressed this same experience. We know intellectually, and by faith, that it is a wonderful time to rejoice in Jesus being raised by the Father. But in spite of that truth, we sometimes just cannot muster an "alleluia" within us no matter how hard we try to find the smile in our spirit. Illness or other bodily changes, tragedy or other anxieties, may prevent us from feeling the enthusiasm proclaimed in the songs, prayers, and messages of Easter.

What if we wake up Easter morning and feel crabby, restless, lonely, sad, pained or discouraged instead of feeling the hope, joy, peace, delight, and new life that the church invites us to experience? One consoling aspect is that Easter is more than a feeling moment. It is a faith moment. It is a time when we bring our whole self to join with others in celebrating a significant fact of our belief, and in so doing we can sometimes catch the spirit of joy from their hearts. At other times, we can enter into their spirit of celebration simply by being bonded, being present with them, knowing with satisfaction that we are at home with Easter's spirit because of the joy in their hearts.

I have discovered yet another way of rejoicing when my feelings do not match the feast's message. It is the gift of recognizing and remembering all the "little Easters" of my life throughout the year.

This discovery of the little Easters came upon me one day in April as a woman told me how extremely discouraged she was because her days were just made up of "little things." that seemed so terribly insignificant and unimportant. During the next several weeks I began to notice all the "insignificant or little things" in my days. As I did so, a quiet surprise happened inside of me. I was amazed by all the little moments or little Easters, those feelings of joy, surprise, amazement, hope, newness, that get clouded by the tough stuff and the daily dyings. (Why is it that it seems to be so much easier to get caught up in the hard things and the struggles than it is to remember the happy moments?) I began to see how I allowed my spirit to get bogged down in anxieties and problems because I did not notice and celebrate the simple, little surprises. I can know little Easters all year long and, if I develop a recognition of and a taste for them, they will deepen my faith in the resurrection even when I do not feel the joy at the time of its celebration.

My little Easters are those moments when I feel hope press against my spirit and I say, "Hooray! God *is* alive and he loves me so much!" My little Easters are those moments when something that has died in me is raised to life again:

— watching and caring for the tiny seeds of marigolds and one day seeing fresh, green shoots break through the soil

— hearing a prayer come from a high school student who's so shy about sharing his God with anyone

— having a kindergarten girl knock on the front door and ask for a cookie

— receiving a letter from a friend who writes, "Hello, I've missed you"

— answering a phone call from a woman I do not know very well and hearing her joy as I accept an invitation to dinner at her home

— hearing my young niece struggle to say "snicklefritz" and her delight when finally pronouncing it correctly

— being given a bouquet of wild flowers picked and saved for me by two happy-hearted senior citizens

It would be so easy to pass these things by or not notice how significant they are to my life. I may not always have a high-in-the-sky feeling when I celebrate Easter but I do know that they provide quiet reassurances that God keeps raising dead parts of my spirit to life. I have the hope that comes from knowing that risen Jesus is not just a bible story. He is here, in my very midst. I have known him in too many little Easters to ever doubt that presence. I have been surprised so often, surprised at how simply the risen Lord is near, at how intensely God visits me, surprised at how much hope simple events have given my heart, surprised at how this hopeful God always re-enters my existence through the people around me.

God is always calling to me, like Jesus called the name of his friend, Mary, in the garden. I, too, can hear the risen one call my name in the garden of my life if only I will listen, if only I will allow my heart to be surprised and amazed by the things of life that bring me joy: love, care, concern, growth, beauty, friendship, faith, courage, mystery, the life events containing any of these are opportunities to re-enter Easter. They are invitations to celebrate the risen Lord every day of our lives. They are calls to look through the disguises of life for God's presence and for God's blessing.

The days of the Easter season will, undoubtedly, be busy for you. I would encourage you to savor them, not let them be drudgery for you. When you rise in the morning, pray an act of faith asking the risen Jesus to bless your rising and your going forth into the Galilee of your ministry. Beg for an awareness of the "little things" of that day.

Before you close your eyes for a night's sleep, recall the day's little Easters: What have been your joyful moments? Have you prayed for the grace of God's re-entry into your life? Have you noticed how Jesus uses other people in your life for his Easter appearances?

Take time to read a scripture passage. Let it be food for your little Easters during the day, keeping you aware of how the risen Lord keeps on being the fullness of life for you.

May you hear the Savior call your name often in your own garden of life. May those moments inspire you to deeper faith, the kind that can carry you through feasts and seasons when your spirit may not know feelings of alleluia.

Scripture Texts for Daily Prayer

Scripture passages for you to read and to pray, to bless your little Easters and to bring you back to life:

Mk 16:1-8   "You are looking for Jesus of Nazareth, who was crucified: He has risen. . . ."

Lk 24:13-35   Jesus brings life to two very discouraged people.

Mk 16:9-14   "But they did not believe her when they heard her say that he was alive and that she had seen him."

Jn 20:1-9   "He saw and he believed."

Lk 24:36-49   The risen Jesus offers peace to his followers.

Jn 20:11-18   Do we hear the Lord call our name in the garden of our lives?

Jn 20:19-31   "Happy are those who have not seen and yet believe."

Rom 6:1-11   How marvelous is my share, even now, in the risen life of Jesus.

Jn 21:1-14   The joy of recognizing the risen one in our midst.

Rom 5:1-11   Nourished by the Spirit, our faith and hope spring from the resurrection and testify to it.

Acts 2:22-28   "You have made known the way of life to me."

Acts 3:1-10   The very name of the glorified Lord creates new life and health.

Acts 13:26-37   "They took him down from the tree and buried him in a tomb. But God raised him from the dead."

Acts 10:34-43   Peter tells the story of Jesus' coming forth from the tomb and what this implies for all his listeners.

Col 2:9-15	Lord, lead me into the fullness of your risen life.
2 Cor 1:8-11	Christian life: hope-filled mystery of dying and rising with Christ.
Jn 15:1-7	Remain with me and you will have life.
Jn 12:20-28	The seed dies before it comes to life; so, too, with Jesus and with us.
Jn 1:1-5	"All that came to be had life in him."
Eph 5:1-16	Life takes on new meaning because of Jesus.
Col 2:6-15	Jesus risen is the source of new life.
1 Cor 15:20-28	In Christ Jesus, all will come to life.
Jn 10:6-10	"I have come so that they may have life and have it to the full."
Jn 11:1-44	"Come out!" Be untombed.
Is 42:5-9	"Thus says God . . . who gave breath to its people and life to the creatures that move in it."
2 Pt 1:3-11	". . . he has given us all the things that we need for life and for true devotion."
2 Cor 4:1-18	We do not lose heart because our inner life is renewed each day.
Sg 2:8-17	"For see, winter is past. . . . The flowers appear on the earth."
Hos 6:1-6	"He will bring us back to life. . . . He will come to us as showers come, like spring rains watering the earth."
Ez 37:1-14	The Lord Yahweh says this to these bones: "I am now going to make breath enter you, and you will live."

A "Little Easter"

the quiet streams of melting snow
have been a source of awakening,
speaking to some deep, inner core
that cries out for definitions in hope.

I take to the street, not the sidewalk,
moving slowly along the watery story:
snowflakes have died under sunshine,
and their bodies trickle quietly along.

the terrible question stops my walking:
why does this death undo my own?
why do flickers of life fill my spirit?

I take to the street, slowly uphill,
listening to the questions within my soul,
listening to the music of the melting.

it's the constancy of the slow-running stream
(all night, all day, the journey continues);
it's the quietness of the movement
(easy to pass by this funeral march of flakes);
it's the sureness with which the water runs
(the tiny stream is yearning to finally fill earth)

thus it is that peace moves in,
destroying deathbeats of my spirit,
conquering all the winter in me.

I breathe Easter before its time,
and my question of hope is lifted high,
melted into the season of life.

Prayer

"Touch me and see for yourselves."
Luke 24:39

Praise to you, my risen Redeemer, who keeps on challenging the doubt in me, who perceives the Thomas in me and allows me those graceful times when I, too, can put my fingers into the signs and wounds of my everyday life and there come in contact with you.

Praise to you, my risen Lord, who keeps on meeting me in the garden of my life, who keeps on calling my name, allowing me to feel loved, blessed and cherished.

Praise to you, risen Jesus, who walks with me on my Emmaus journeys, coaxing the ache out of me, comforting and strengthening me with the intimate presence of yourself.

Praise to you, my risen Savior, who surprises me on the sandy beaches of my so often planned and programmed life, inviting me to come and taste what you have prepared. Time after time, you nourish me with all that I need to carry your risen presence with me, wherever I go and to whomever I meet.

Questions for Journal Keeping

Week 1   What do you most wish to resurrect in your life this Easter season? (Is there a Lazarus in you that needs to be untombed?)

Week 2   In what events, people, situations of the past week have you heard the risen Lord call your name in the garden of your life, in the Galilee of your ministry?

Week 3   Is your spirit open to wonder and to surprise? What might be keeping you from entering into the surprise of life's "little things"?

Week 4   In reflecting over the past four weeks, what have been the most significant "little Easters" of your month? What has made them so significant?

❧ MAY

The Heart
of the Seed

"Seed-Song"

I am the seed
so small, so dry,
lifted in the hand
of the silent Sower.

into the earth
I fearfully fall,
darkness covers me,
silence surrounds me.

the terror of my heart
is the only sound
to keep me company.

all that is me
huddles together
trying desperately
not to surrender
any part of self.

"why was I planted?"
I cry out.
"why am I here?"
I entreat.
"take me out into light;
I cannot bear
this deathly dark."

I weary. I weaken.
the days become long.
I can no longer fight.
I surrender
in this lonely place
of waiting.

quietly I sense
a penetrating warmth;
it surrounds me;
it fills me
and blesses my pain.

in a moment
of peacefulness
I forget my fear.

I let go of my self
and suddenly
the husk that holds me
weakens and breaks.

"No!" I scream.
I am losing my self,
but it is too late.
the husk is cracked;
I cannot be contained.

it is then
that I sense a power
deep inside of me,
encouraging me:
"let go. let go. let go."

it is an energy
that pushes the husk
until it falls away.

as it slips aside
my eyes behold color.
ah! can it be?
a tiny glimpse of green!

"how could that be?"
I marvel,
"there was never green
in the heart of me."

yet, it is there;
each day
it slowly stretches upwards
to where the warm
seems to be.

I become less of a seed.
I am losing my self
but the pain I once knew
is lost in surprise;
something wonderful
is greening and growing
deep within my heart.

days go quickly now.
I become one
with the small stem of life.

oh! the glorious moment
when, ah, breath of Spring
fast fills my face.
I move through the hard earth
and taste the world which awaits my arrival.

from within my tender shoot
comes a soft sound.
I listen. I hear.
it is a song to the Sower:

O Sower of seeds,
did you always see
this gift of green
that was hiding in me?

O Sower of seeds,
how came you to prize
the beauty within
that I hid from my eyes?

O Sower of seeds,
the husk has been broken;
all praise to you
for helping me open.

Accept now my praise,
my thankfulness, too,
for the seed you have sown
and the gift that you grew.

May you lead me to others
who await your good word,
so the seeds within them
can awake and be heard.

amen! alleluia!

If you drive along a country road on a sunny day in early May, you will most surely see tractors rolling across the farmlands, their huge plows digging up the ground, turning it under and lifting up new goodness. You will see farmers with their planters setting the seed in the freshness of the soil. You will see the beautiful quilted look of the earth—furrows of brown lines left from the plowing, pastures green with growing.

When I look at the earth so lovely in springtime readiness, I reflect on what it is like to have my heart ready for the word of God. I, too, must be open to the turning over and the turning under of last year's harvest. I, too, must be willing to have the sharp blades of life's difficulties slice through my convictions and have them blended in faith. I, too, must allow my spirit's rough edges to be smoothed so that God's seed can take root in me, so that the word of God will be deeply implanted in my every thought and action. Most of all, I must believe in my potential to receive the word of God and my potential to become an ever more whole human being, recognizing and developing the gifts which the sower has given me.

A seed has so much potential, despite a rather insignificant appearance. We can hardly believe that life can come forth from such a dry, dead-looking thing. Yet, deep within its heart can be a glorious sunflower or a delicious ear of corn. A seed can hold all the potential in the world but unless it is planted, it cannot grow. A maple seed can't just hang onto a tree and produce another maple tree. A tomato seed can't stay inside the tomato and expect to bring forth another red juicy fruit. Seeds have to be sown. They need to fall from plants and be washed by the rain into soil, be carried by birds or wind, travel on the fur of animals, or be harvested by humans and sown by machines. Some seeds are gently held in a human hand and placed softly in a garden row.

Then the challenge is up to the seed. All the warmth and water in the world won't create another plant unless the seed's husk is broken and shed. Only then will that wonderful new shoot of life begin to burst forth. An acorn is always an acorn until it cracks and the shell is gone. Then it begins to be an oak tree. What a risk it is to venture forth from the security of the shell!

The inner home of humans is a lot like the heart of a seed. Like seeds, we have a great potential for receiving the word of God, for becoming who we are meant to be. Deep within us are many gifts and virtues that have never been sown. They just lie there, seemingly dry and lifeless. No one has ever come along and believed in the seed. No one has planted it in rich, good soil. No one has ever given it warmth and water. No one has said, "Yes, I think you can do it!" or "Go ahead. I'll be there to support you." or "Have you ever thought of how good you are at . . .?" Until we affirm another's gift, that person is not really sure he or she has that gift. The best cook isn't sure about how good a cook she is until she hears that "mmmm" from a contented eater. The best parent isn't sure he's done a good job unless his children say, "I really like the way you . . ." or "Thank you for. . . ."

It is not only others who need to affirm and believe in our potential, we ourselves must believe in what lies within us. We also have to believe in our deep storehouse of giftedness. The more we believe in this treasury the more we will be willing to risk "cracking open the husk" of that potential. One of my favorite posters says: "Every day we should do something that will expand us; we should win little victories over our fears that will widen the world and our lives. We will gradually learn in this way about the undreamed of potentialities which we had all the time but never used," (John Powell, S. J.).

What keeps "the undreamed of potentialities" from growing in our lives? Often our fears. Sometimes we do not let the word of God take seed in us because of our selfishness but I venture that much more often we keep the husk on the shell because of our fears. Deep inside of us these fears take form in little messages that scare the seed:

—"I can't do it."

—"What will they say?"

—"They'll think I'm stupid."

—"They won't like me."

—"She can do it better than I can."

—"What if I fail?"

Fear of what others may think of us keeps us from reaching out to someone who may really need our gifts of listening and compassion. Fear of what might be asked of us keeps us from letting people know what our gifts are, and thus we miss being of service in a parish or neighborhood. Fear for our own reputation keeps us from being with certain types of people or from speaking on their behalf when there's a need to do so. Fear of failure keeps us from risking a new job or meeting people who might bring us more to life. Fear of facing our inadequacies keeps us from communicating on more than a surface level and thus, we abort the deeper friendships or love waiting to be born. Fear of the unknown keeps us in our own little world, like a seed lying dormant, refusing to germinate, missing the wonders of what we could become.

May is an excellent time to face our fears and recognize more of our potential for wholeness. It is an excellent time to encourage that growth in others. The word of God is waiting to come to birth in a more total way in each of us. We are meant for the glory of God. We are made in that image and likeness in the way that an apple seed is made for the fullness of an apple tree. We have the potential to live the values and the virtues of the scriptures. The beatitudes seeded in us are the beautiful qualities named in 1 Corinthians 13. The compassion of Jesus waits in us to give birth as do the reaching out of his care and the risk-taking of his truth-bearing.

Our hearts are the soil for these wonderful "seeds." As you celebrate springtime, take a seed in your hand. Hold it carefully before you. Bless it with your presence and your prayer. Let your prayer arise to the sower of all seeds. Pray that you can call forth the gifts of one other person this springtime. Pray that you may do so by letting him or her know the good you see within them. Say more "thank-yous" and fewer "who cares." Appreciate more and complain less. Take more time with people so you can discover their hidden gifts. Never give up on the seeds of goodness in others. (Radishes sprout very quickly while beets are slower to germinate. Each has its own time of growth.)

Take a spring stroll. Find something green and growing. Observe little shoots of new growth. Reflect on your need to be open to the seed of God's word and your potential for goodness. Praise God for all the growth you see in the green of spring and in the green of your own heart.

You might wish to plant a seed or two. Nurture them and watch them grow. As you see them each day, you will be reminded of the seed within you that is carrying so much potential for giftedness and growth.

Scripture Texts for Daily Prayer

"What the sower is sowing is the word."
Mark 4:14

The seed of . . .

Mk 1:16-20	following Jesus.
Mk 1:29-34	healing.
Mk 1:35-39	solitude.
Mk 1:40-45	sympathy.
Mk 2:1-12	forgiveness.
Mk 2:15-17	repentance.
Mk 3:31-35	the will of God.
Mk 4:1-20	the word of God.
Mk 4:24-34	listening.
Mk 4:35-41	faith.
Mk 5:1-20	peace.

Mk 5:21-35	inner power.
Mk 6:7-13	simplicity.
Mk 6:53-56	healing touch.
Mk 7:24-30	persistence.
Mk 8:1-10	compassion.
Mk 8:14-21	inner vision.
Mk 8:27-30	truth.
Mk 8:34-9:1	discipleship.
Mk 9:2-8	glory.
Mk 9:14-29	prayer.
Mk 9:33-37	servanthood.
Mk 9:38-41	belonging to the Christ.
Mk 10:17-22	invitation.
Mk 10:46-52	courage.
Mk 11:10-25	praise.
Mk 12:28-34	love.
Mk 12:41-44	generosity.
Mk 14:3-9	caring.
Mk 16:1-8	proclamation.

A Creed for the Sowing of Seeds

"A man throws seed on the land. Night and day, while he sleeps, when he is awake, the seed is sprouting and growing; how, he does not know."

Mark 4:26-28

I believe that this is one of the earth's finest moments, that the sun lifting yellows and greens into life of tiny poplar leaves is much like God's own Spirit of love lifting life into me.

I believe that the Word of God has many times been planted in my life, often because of another who received the seed in ready soil, brought forth a harvest, and shared that goodness with me.

I believe that the call to be a sower of the Word is a privilege and a blessing, that no one can ever earn the right or claim the duty, that it is a gift freely given and a ministry to be constantly celebrated in gratitude.

I believe that great things can come forth from even the tiniest seed planted in love and cared for tenderly in the heart of another.

I believe that usually only God knows what sprouting and greening will come from the Word planted through my ministry. I am content in knowing that I have tried, with the Sower's grace, to seed that Word in faith and with joy.

I believe that even the most insignificant aspects of life can be the seed of God's gifting, that deeper faith can root and mature in very ordinary soil.

I believe that some dying of seed has to take place before it can give itself over to life, that every heart has its germination time, its dark moment, before the future hallowedness of harvest comes.

I believe that it takes much patience to sow a seed, to freely give it away to the heart of earth, to allow it to take root and to grow in its own good time.

I believe that my life will always know its season of hope, that I will find flowers after every finality of ice and snow, that I will find green, growing things after every harsh, barren reign of winter's rage.

and most of all . . .

I believe in the Sower of all seeds, in the God of Springtime, in the Giver of all good and growing things, my Lord and my God!

Prayer

O God, in whose image and likeness I am made, as much as I believe that the abundance of your goodness is strewn all through this heart of mine, I still struggle with that truth. I find myself wondering about my inner growth, if there is anything really happening there: Am I full of life? Am I growing? Why is it so dark sometimes? Why can't I see better what kind of growth is taking place? Is it all worth it? Who am I becoming?

When the earth of my soul cries out for water, for refreshment and for nourishment, it is then that these questions seem most to threaten my beliefs. So much dryness there is all within me, God. I am seeded in such seemingly arid soil that I wonder if the green of goodness will ever appear above the ground. Yet, amid all that dry earth, there is a quiet stirring, a drawing, a silent movement that encourages me to believe in the potential within me. I need only to trust you which does not mean the questions will end. I need only to allow you to take hold of me, as the earth takes hold of the silence of a seed.

I trust you, O God, in whose image and likeness I am made. I trust you to come along some silent night, bringing life to the seed of my soul, bringing waters to wake my dead. Amen.

Questions for Journal Keeping

Week 1   You are the soil in which the word of God is to be rooted. How would you describe your soil?

Week 2   We are made "in the image and likeness of God" (Gn 1:26). How do you see yourself as made in "the image and likeness of God?" (What does this mean to you in your life now?)

Week 3   You are the seed, bearing so much potential for growth. What is already green and growing in your life? Can you name some of the dormant gifts in you that have been begging to be born?

Week 4   Read and pray the "Seed-Song." After you imagine yourself to be the seed in dark soil coming to life, write about the feelings that you have. As you reflect on your seed-song experience, what insights did you have about yourself, about God, about the process of life and growth?

⚓ JUNE

The Encircling Rainbow

a strong rainbow pours itself out,
bending the eastern sky with glory,
it brings with it a powerful beauty
to soothe my needy heart with hope.

and I do believe I hear the sun
wild with wonder and rejoicing,
laughing at the once-darkened sky
now parted in colored splendor.

I remember then the One who came,
who broke our stormy dark apart,
and shook despairing hearts with hope;
this one told truth of things beyond
and gave us more than gold.

this rainbow filling late-June sky
touches more than just the earth;
it makes its mark within my deep
and lets my heart look up in hope.

One evening in early June, I heard a knock on the door. It was a time when I was very tired, when things all seemed to be happening at once. I felt a deadness, an inability to be enthused or excited. I wondered what all the running and busyness was worth, and I felt very discouraged about my presence among those around me.

I went to the door thinking someone would ask me to do "one more thing." Instead, I discovered a friend from the next town telling me of something that I needed to see. He said excitedly, "I was just driving by and I had to stop and see if you were home and if you had noticed it. There's something wonderful outside. Come and see!" His voice and the joy in his eyes made me hurry out to the sidewalk. There in the eastern sky was one of the most magnificent rainbows that I have ever seen. The color and the fullness of the bow were beautiful. Looking at it I felt overwhelmed by glory. It was as though God was circling the world with loving arms.

I stood there for a long time, amazed by beauty, caught up in the wonder of nature. As I walked into the house I felt something new inside of me. I named it "hope and happiness." My tiredness had quietly been replaced with a sense of peace and beauty. My questions about my crazy calendar had been stilled with the reassurance of God's nearness. My heart was happy with the thought that someone cared enough about me to deliberately stop and invite me to see a rainbow.

Since that rainbow moment, I have thought many a time about the experience. The rainbow has a long history as a sign of hope on the spiritual journey. In the story of Noah the rainbow is a symbol of the promise that God made to the people who were saved from the earth's destruction. There is a hopeful power in the story of Noah, the tale of a person who braved long, lonely moments, wondering what life was worth when all that he knew of it was being destroyed. He must have questioned how he and his family would survive. The moment when Noah opened the window and sent out the dove is special and hope-filled. Noah is everyone of us when we sit in our discouragement, calling out to God or others; "Tell me about hope; give me reason to believe; help me to trust in the goodness of life; enable me to find my courage and to be enthused about life again; tell me about the meaning of life." What a profound confirmation of hope it was for Noah when the dove came back bearing the tiny sprig of green in its beak, the green which said: "Welcome into new life. Here is a gift of hope for you. Believe in the future. Trust what is to come. All will be well with you."

Then, as a significant blessing, as a sign of the truth of all that Noah believed about the future, God spoke to him and said:

> "See, I establish my Covenant with you, and with your descendents after you. . . . Here is the sign of the Covenant I make between myself and you and every living creature with you for all generations: I set my bow in the clouds and it shall be a sign of the Covenant between me and the earth. When I gather the clouds over the earth and the bow appears in the clouds, I will recall the Covenant between myself and you and every living creature of every kind. And so the waters shall never again become a flood to destroy all things of flesh. When the bow is in the clouds I shall see it and call to mind the lasting Covenant between God and every living creature of every kind that is found on the earth" (Gn 9:7-16).

The rainbow has thus become a sign of the promises God makes to all of us who go on searching, struggling, dreaming and believing while on the human journey.

Rainbow callers are people who announce hope to others—like the dove returning with a sprig of green, or the rainbow announcing hope to Noah. Sometimes it is hard to think of hope being announced when our world is filled with war, when so many lives are filled with pain and conflict, struggle and darkness.

To hope is more than just to wish for something. It is

to yearn for and to dream something so much that we really believe it can be, that it will happen even though the odds may be against it. To hope is to have a strong, clear, positive vision of the future. To hope is to know the God of hope, the God of promise, the one who has already taken us out of darkness into wonderful light. In Hannah Hurnard's *Hinds Feet on High Places,* the Shepherd asks Much Afraid: "Do you love me enough to be able to trust me completely?" That question is the core of hope; it asks: Have we fallen in love enough with the God of hope that we can trust he will always be with us no matter what our trials and tribulations may be? Do we love enough to send out a dove and to look for signs of rainbows in the sky?

Trust is a gradual, growing thing. We keep giving ourselves to God and then, keep taking ourselves back. We need to be very aware of keeping our hope alive, of drawing our trust to greater depths. Hope doesn't just happen. It has to be nurtured in the human heart. How do we nurture hope? How do we keep on being rainbow callers?

Three things that keep hope alive in my heart, that keep the rainbow vivid in my life, are: beauty moments, truth touches, and value bonds.

A *beauty moment* can rekindle my hope in the goodness of God. Something so ordinarily beautiful as smile wrinkles around some aging eyes or as lovely as a morning star filling a dawn sky can assure me of the blessing of God within the human spirit.

Truth touches are those inner stirrings (I am sure it is God) that continually remind me that life is worth living and that God's promises are true. Hope comes leaping out in such scripture passages as Colossians 1:12-20: "The Father . . . has taken us out of the power of darkness and created a place for us in the Kingdom of the Son whom he loves." This *truth touch* helps me believe far beyond today and the difficult moments it may hold. I find truth touches in scripture and in the voices and the written words of others.

Value bonds assure me that I am not in this life

alone. Others believe and hope as I do. It is always so encouraging to meet others who hunger and yearn for some of the values I believe in at the core of my being. It is important that I take time to find these people and to share my own encouragement with them, too. Each one of us needs someone who will knock on the door of our heart, someone who sees rainbows, has hope, believes in the God of promises, someone who invites us out of our own world of anxiety, confusion and doubt. People all around us need us to be rainbow callers for them, to remind them about the gift of God in their lives, to hold out the treasure of hope to them, to call them to see beauty in a God-given world often caught in ugliness to enable them to find meaning in their common moments, be they happy or difficult.

I believe that if we are to be hope-filled people, if we are to be rainbow callers, we need to fall deeply in love with God and treasure the promises we hear in the scriptures. We need to experience laughter, to delight in life's incongruities. We need to have a time each day to recall God's presence and believe again in the wonders and beauties around us. We also need to keep searching for people who believe and hope for what we hunger for in our hearts.

This month read the daily newspaper with an eye for some hopeful news. Circle and cut out these items and place them where you will see them often.

Each evening before you sleep, reflect on your day. Jot down one thing that was a sign of hope for you. Keep adding to your list all during the month of June. At the end of the month, post this list or keep it in your bible. Let it be a hopeful sign to you, like the little rainbow on a cloudy day. "See the rainbow and praise its maker" (Sir 43:11). Lift up your heart in hope and share that hope with others.

Scripture Texts for Daily Prayer

Gn 9:8-17 — "I set my bow in the clouds and it shall be a sign of the Covenant between me and the earth."

Ez 1:26-28 — ". . . like a bow in the clouds on rainy days. . . . It was something that looked like the glory of Yahweh."

Col 1:24-27 — "The mystery is Christ among you, your hope of glory."

Rom 5:1-11 — "This hope is not deceptive, because the love of God has been poured into our hearts by the Holy Spirit. . . ."

Rom 1:1-15 — ". . . to find encouragement among you from our common faith."

Rom 4:18-25 — "Though it seemed Abraham's hope could not be fulfilled, he hoped and he believed."

Rom 8:18-27 — "I think that what we suffer in this life can never be compared to the glory, as yet unrevealed, which is waiting for us."

Rom 8:31-39 — "With God on our side who can be against us?"

Rom 10:14021 — "The footsteps of those who bring good news is a welcome sound."

Rom 12:3-13 — "Work for the Lord with untiring effort and with great earnestness of spirit. If you have hope, this will make you cheerful."

Rom 15:1-6 — "Everything that was written long ago in the scriptures was meant to teach us something about hope."

Rom 15:7-13 — "May the God of hope bring you such joy and peace in your faith that the power of the Holy Spirit will remove all bounds to hope."

Eph 1:3-14	"And you too have been stamped with the seal of the Holy Spirit of the Promise."
Heb 6:9-20	". . . take a firm grip on the hope that is held out to us."
Heb 10:19-25	"Let us keep firm in the hope we profess, because the one who made the promise is faithful."
1 Pt 3:13-17	"Always have your answer ready for people who ask you the reason for the hope that you all have."
1 Cor 15:9-19	"If our hope in Christ has been for this life only, we are the most unfortunate of all people."
2 Cor 1:1-11	"And he saved us from dying, as he will save us again; yes, that is our firm hope in him. . . ."
2 Cor 6:1-10	"We beg you once again not to neglect the grace of God that you have received."
Jer 29:4-14	"I know the plans I have in mind for you—it is Yahweh who speaks—. . . reserving a future full of hope for you."
Jer 31:8-14	"I will change their mourning into gladness, comfort them, give them joy after their troubles."
Zep 3:14-18	"You have no more evil to fear. . . . Yahweh your God is in your midst."
1 Thess 3:6-13	". . . your faith has been a great comfort to us."
1 Thes 5:1-11	"So give encouragement to each other, and keep strengthening one another, as you do already."
2 Thes 2:13-17	". . . such inexhaustible comfort and such sure hope. . . ."

Eph 1:15-23 "May he enlighten the eyes of your mind so that you can see what hope his call holds for you."

Col 1:3-14 "You will have in you the strength, based on his own glorious power, never to give in, but to bear anything joyfully."

Ti 1:1-4 ". . . to give them the hope of the eternal life that was promised so long ago by God."

the demon of discouragement
trips me up in hectic times,
takes my heart apart
and dumps out all my hope.

the demon of discouragement
points fingers at my weakness,
jaws his mouth at all my errors
and threatens to undo me.

the demon of discouragement
despises rainbows, relishes rancor,
fights to hold my moody darkness
and loves to see me weary.

the demon of discouragement
fails to have the last laugh, though,
for I've too many people of promise
whose loves outlast my struggles.

Prayer

Dear Lord,

Today is one of those days when I want to reach out with you and touch a bright, distant star, to hold it in a quiet, loving way, knowing it symbolizes many dreams that I have known because of you.

Dear Lord,

Today is one of those days when I want to give you my tears and let you hold them in your heart, knowing that they are the sign of the many ways I am still not yours.

Dear Lord,

Today is one of those days when I pray you'll lift me to your cheek and whisper again your love to me, telling me that you still want me and that I'll always find a welcome there.

Dear Lord,

Today is one of those days when I come before you and stand with you. I look into your face. I feel the pull of my heart toward yours, a pull not unlike that of a rainbow glow as it fills the sky on a rainy day. I know in this moment of heart tug how much you care and hope for me, and I know how deeply I do love you.

Questions for Journal Keeping

Week 1   What does it mean for you to belong to the God of promises? How has this God been faithful to you?

Week 2   On your hopeless days, in your discouraged times, what keeps hope from happening in your heart?

Week 3   Name discouraged and distressful aspects of your life. Where or to whom would you most want to bring the hope of God?

Week 4   What is the hope that God has given to you this month? Describe that hope. Write your prayer of praise to the maker of rainbows, to the giver of hope.

You Are a Letter From Jesus

You are a letter from Christ.
2 Corinthians 3:3

in the mailbox of my life
I've found many forms of letters
but the ones I've most rejoiced in
are the ones sent from my Lord.

they look most ordinary
that no one would suspect
they bear the blessed message
of the truth about my heart.

some letters bring me challenge
to forego my hardened ways;
some letters invite happiness
and promise new delight.

some letters gift my days with hope
when all the world seems dark;
some letters bear tough questions
regarding weaknesses and sin.

some letters send me healing
when my heart is weary;
some letters speak of loving
and of giving beyond cost.

some letters make me wonder
how I ever could refuse,
for they are letters of proposal
for a love life with my God.

I know that I'll keep coming
to the mailbox of my life,
because the letters tell of Jesus
and pursue me with his truth.

Yesterday I went to the mailbox and there was a happy surprise awaiting me: a long overdue letter from one of my favorite people. I immediately took it to my room, sat in my comfy rocking chair, and read the contents with great fondness. As I read its two full pages I felt tears begin to surface in my heart and fill my eyes. Little drops of joy fell upon my cheeks. I closed my eyes and held the words of the letter close to my moment of happiness. It was one of those times when I realized how much God gives me in the treasure of friendship and in its long-lastingness.

As I reflected on the letter I recognized that it was easy to be in touch with the inside story of my friend's heart. For she wrote not only of external events but also of the internal events of her life, her many shades of feelings and insights over the past weeks. The tears of gratitude came because I was overwhelmed with the gift of being able to read someone else's heart and see so much wonder, beauty, and goodness.

I think that is what it is like to be a "letter from Christ" which the author of Corinthians writes of in Chapter 3. It is to look into someone else's life and to see there the wonder, beauty and goodness of our God:

> You are yourselves our letter, written in our hearts, that anybody can see and read, and it is plain that you are a letter from Christ, drawn up by us, and written not with ink but with the Spirit of the living God, not on stone tablets but on the tablets of your living hearts (2 Cor 3:2-3).

A letter can say many things to the receiver and many things about the sender. When we receive a letter, the handwriting, the content, and the way it is worded all indicate information about the author: How does this person begin the letter?—warmly, fondly, happily, sadly, angrily? Does he or she take a long time to get to the heart of the matter or is there any heart to the matter? What is the farewell like? What about the handwriting?—slow and

methodical, sweeping and luxurious, stately and digni-
fied, sketchy and hastily penned, tiny and painstakingly
written?

What about the messages?—excited, calm, worried,
sad, elated, searching, joyful, wondering, daydreamy, intense, personal, containing good-byes, hellos, love devel-
opments, love expressions? Sometimes letters only say
surface things, mentioning external events and places or
situations. At other times, the letters have messages that
easily put us deeply in touch with the senders. We perceive quickly who they are and how they are. (This is the
kind of letter that the author of Corinthians intended.) To
be a letter from Christ is to be so transparent that the
goodness of our inner selves is seen, the qualities of Jesus shine forth in us like messages shine from a letter
penned from the depths of one's heart.

Across all of our lives are "marks" of the Lord
whether we "see" them or not—marks that make us a letter from Jesus. We wear messages on our personalities
about what we know and believe regarding the person of
Jesus. What is it to have the qualities of Jesus written on
our hearts? Think of how powerful and influential and
significant that can be. Can you imagine yourself to be a
letter from the Christ? Can you believe that you are a
message sent to tell others about Jesus?

If we are to be an open letter in which others recognize the Lord because of what is written in our own hearts
and on our lives, then we must have his qualities etched
on our very being. We must constantly strive to know Jesus, to know his gospel goodness, so that we can have it
as part of our life's message. We must come to know this
Jesus whose letter we are, to renew our acquaintance
with this one whose godly qualities shone through his
deeply human person. We must come close to this Jesus
who was so taken up with his Father's love that those
around him recognized him as the one "nearest to the Father's heart" (Jn 1:18). They saw that the power and
goodness working through his ministry was that of a divine source. Jesus was truly a letter from the Father just
as we are meant to be a letter from the Son. Jesus turned

to the Father to learn from him. He knew the Father's goodness was being manifested through his own life because he kept returning to the Father in prayer, thus filling his heart with a message that could be read in every fiber of his being. So, too, we with Jesus—we must keep returning to him in prayer so that we can know him well, so that we can invite his qualities into our own lives and wear them on our hearts.

Who is the Christ we are called to reflect? If we look constantly to the scriptures we can recognize that Jesus is someone who:

- —experienced solitude as a source of strength
- —allowed compassion to move through his glances and his actions
- —opened his heart to the unwanted
- —moved beyond the comfortable and took risks
- —listened to and took notice of the concerns in others' lives
- —had great confidence in the strength and care of the Father for us
- —offered peace and healing to wounded ones
- —shared a love that stretched far beyond himself
- —encouraged simplicity and single-heartedness for his followers
- —looked upon others with deep love
- —gave of self even in great tiredness
- —turned always to the Father in moments of need
- —carried a presence that encouraged others
- —lived the life of a suffering servant for the sake of the kingdom
- —acknowledged and praised the faith of others
- —extended forgiveness readily and constantly
- —shared Eucharist as a bond of love
- —struggled to do the Father's will

—desired and sought the truth for himself and for others

—accepted and rejoiced in the resurrection moments

These are some of the qualities of Jesus that I have found while praying the gospels. You will find others that are meaningful to you because of who you discover Jesus to be in your life.

As we assume and deepen these qualities and as we become more and more of his letter, we will become more and more transparent. We will be more open, sincere, and honest with others, and they will be able to see more and more clearly how much of Jesus is written on our hearts. Jesus praised Nathanael when he met him because Nathanael had no guile; he was without deceit. He was someone on whose heart the message of Jesus could easily be transcribed and sent. Jesus praised children, too, for their coming to him. Children are also transparent and easily allow others to see their feelings and thoughts. Like Nathanael, like the children whom Jesus praised, we too, must be open, must allow people to know us if the gospel characteristics of Jesus are to be seen there. Let people come into your heart, help them to meet the one you know and love. Be a letter from the Christ.

This July remind yourself often that "you must live your whole life according to the Christ you have received" (Col 2:6) and that you are to be a letter from Jesus to all those in your life. Take the time to know Jesus better. Renew your friendship and deepen your love for him by reading the scriptures, by listening to music that sings about him, by finding spiritual reading that tells of him. Look for the letters from Jesus that others are to you. And remember,"there is only Christ: he is everything and he is in everything" (Col 3:11).

Scripture Texts for Daily Prayer

Eph 2:1-10	"We are God's work of art, created in Christ Jesus to live the good life. . . ."
Eph 3:1-13	"You will have some idea of the depths that I see in the mystery of Christ."
Eph 4:1-16	"Bear with one another charitably, in complete selflessness, gentleness and patience."
Eph 4:17-32	"Be friends with one another, and kind, forgiving each other as readily as God forgave you in Christ."
1 Jn 1:1-4	". . . the Word who is life—this is our subject."
1 Jn 2:3-11	". . . living the same kind of life as Christ lived."
1 Jn 3:1-9	". . . to live a holy life is to be holy just as he is holy."
Gal 2:15-21	"I live now not with my own life but with the life of Christ who lives in me."
1 Thes 1:1-10	"This has made you the great example to all believers."
1 Tm 6:11-16	"You must aim to be saintly and religious, filled with faith and love, patient and gentle."
2 Tm 1:6-18	"So you are never to be ashamed of witnessing to the Lord. . . ."
1 Cor 1:1-9	"The witness to Christ has indeed been strong among you. . . ."
1 Cor 2:1-9	". . . the only knowledge I claimed to have was about Jesus, and only about him as the crucified Christ."

1 Cor 2:10-16	"But we are those who have the mind of Christ."
1 Cor 4:1-13	"People must think of us as Christ's servants, stewards entrusted with the mysteries of God."
2 Cor 2:14-17	"Thanks be to God who, wherever he goes, makes us, in Christ, partners of his triumph, and through us is spreading the knowledge of himself. . . ."
2 Cor 3:1-11	"You are a letter from Christ. . . ."
2 Cor 4:1-6	"For it is not ourselves that we are preaching, but Christ Jesus as the Lord. . . ."
Phil 1:3-11	"I am quite certain that the One who began this good work in you will see that it is finished. . . ."
Phil 1:12-26	"Life to me, of course, is Christ."
Phil 1:27-30	"Avoid anything in your everyday lives that would be unworthy of the gospel of Christ."
Phil 2:1-11	"In your minds you must be the same as Christ Jesus."
Phil 2:12-18	"You will shine in the world like bright stars because you are offering it the word of life."
Phil 3:8-16	"I believe nothing can happen that will outweigh the supreme advantage of knowing Christ Jesus my Lord."
Col 1:24-29	"The mystery is Christ among you."
Col 2:6-8	"You must live your whole life according to the Christ you have received— Jesus the Lord."
Col 3:1-4	"The life you have is hidden with Christ in God."

Col 3:5-17   "Let the message of Christ, in all its richness, find a home with you."

Heb 1:1-4   "He (Jesus) is the radiant light of God's glory and the perfect copy of his nature. . . ."

Heb 12:1-4   "Let us not lose sight of Jesus. . . ."

Yes
to you, Jesus

as you offer me your love
as you letter my life with yourself
as you encourage my transparency
as you ask for my honesty
as you desire my everything
as you speak through all I do
as you continue my transformation
as you challenge my weaknesses
as you bless my giftedness
as you take who I am
into your loving embràce

Yes
to you, Jesus

as you catch me up in your arms
as you fire me with your truth
as you seal me with your goodness
as you bless me with the blessing
that only your Father can give

Prayer

Jesus

I am drawn to you this morning
    drawn to you as the gentle loving one
            as the generous one
            as the welcoming one
            as the prayerful one
            as the one who is closest to the
               Father's heart
            as the one sealed with the
               Father's love
            as the one knowing deep within
               your heart
            that your work was to proclaim
               the Kingdom

Jesus

how I want to know you
how I want to take a stand about you in my life
            to surrender myself to you
            to belong to you
            to treasure the belief that I have in you

but my love is weak
    my faith is restless and so often taken for granted
    my self gets in the way and so often blocks you out

O Lord Jesus,

on days when I am especially forgetful
                    unmindful
                    of you

lead me gently away with you
as you led your disciples away with you

reach out to me
teach me about you
and tell me again how much you love me
              who you are
              what it is you ask of me
              that you are all I need

O Lord Jesus

> I stand before you this morning
> in awe of the treasure that you are
> and I bless the gracious Father of all
> who sent you into our midst

Amen.

Questions for Journal Keeping

Week 1 "But you . . . who do you say that I am?" (Mk 8:28). Who is Jesus to you? If someone asked you to speak of your relationship with Jesus, what would you say?

Week 2 What is there about Jesus that especially draws you to love him? (What qualities of Jesus do you most appreciate?)

Week 3 "You are a letter from Christ . . ." (2 Cor 3:3). Describe yourself as a letter from the Christ. What is written "on the tablet of your living heart"?

Week 4 What are the most significant insights and/or feelings you have had during this month of prayer on being a letter of Christ Jesus?

♣ AUGUST

The Fearful
Heart

silent August night
the words I'd long held
surged out in whisper;
almost as though rustle
of the forests' oak leaves
bid the truth be told;
"I am so afraid."

words of truth, air-suspended,
softened by tender-rounded moon,
sparkled on by a million stars.
suddenly night seemed so bright.

the wind that rustled oak leaves
was wind moving through me.
the tiny trickling stream
was bidding me to kneel,
to be humble-poor before Holy,
to lay my overwhelming fear
in gentle, outstretched arms.

oh, for a moment, swept up in God,
stilled, awed, and quieted.

this Presence is Holy, Holy, Holy.

God has taken my fearful heart
and wrapped it in deep Love.

Have you ever thought about all the time we spend worrying? Mark Twain said that most of the things we worry about never happen. But we go on worrying anyhow. When we have special plans or a trip to take, we worry about the weather, if we'll have a good time or if we'll forget something. When we are in a new or different situation, we worry about our appearance or what we will say. If we have good health we worry about becoming ill, if we have poor health we worry about getting well again. We worry about money, and about how we spend our time. We concern ourselves with security, about being a success. We worry about relationships and about children growing up. We become anxious about being on time, looking good, finding fulfillment, being faithful, and ever so many other things.

Yet worrying keeps us from being free, from noticing and enjoying life's goodness. It focuses on what is unknown, or on what we think will soon be there to torment, shame, or haunt us. Worrying saps away our inner energy because we spend so much time tossing and turning over the "what ifs" and the "maybes." Worrying distracts us from our vision, our goals and dreams. It shakes fingers at us and causes us to distrust ourselves. Worrying eats the heart out of peace and tends to keep us occupied with ourselves instead of with God and the people of God.

In a beautiful little book, *Making All Things New,* Henri Nouwen points to worrying as a major hindrance of spiritual growth:

> One of the most notable characteristics of worrying is that it fragments our lives. The many things to do, to think about, to plan for, the many people to remember, to visit, or to talk with, the many causes to attack or defend, all these pull us apart and make us lose our center. Worrying causes us to be "all over the place," but seldom at home. One way to express the spiritual crisis of our time is to say that most of

us have an address but cannot be found there. We know where we belong, but we keep being pulled away in many directions, as if we were still homeless. "All these other things" keep demanding our attention. They lead us so far from home that we eventually forget our true address, that is, the place where we can be addressed.

A good question to ask is: "Why do I worry?" and "What do I worry about?" The many reasons why we give in to this chronic disorder of the spirit include

—A lack of belief in how much God deeply and personally cares for us.

—A persistent attitude that says we can do it all by ourselves, without God's power at work in us. This is a response to life which emphasizes, "I'll manage it by myself" instead of a gospel response of "Let what you have said be done to me" (Lk 1:38).

—A difficulty in accepting the reality that not all of life will be positive, that life bears the marks and smudges of our own and others' human weaknesses, a Pollyanna approach which insists that life must always be fair, comfortable and serene.

—A poor memory which often or quickly forgets that growth can happen through both success and failure.

Another major cause of worry is being afraid of the consequences of our "what ifs" and "maybes." Fear can paralyze us just like a stroke can paralyze the body. I remember visiting a woman in her mid-fifties in a rehabilitation center. I was appalled and saddened to see what a stroke did to a once alert and independent person. It took so much effort for her to reach a stiff, thin arm up to wipe the tears clinging to the corner of her eye. It took all her energy to try to pronounce just one word. I stood by her side, trying to interpret her slurred whispers and I wept for her in that terrible frustration and powerlessness. I thought of how tragic and alone she was in her paralysis, yearning to communicate but unable to do so.

Like physical paralysis, interior paralysis can be just as traumatic and painful. Sometimes we are unable to act or are immobilized in energizing our lives because we have given in to deep fears. They keep us from being free, from having peace in our hearts. They hold us back from joy and from giving our best selves to others. Fears box us in, hold others out, and most of all keep us from knowing the beautiful, tender and good within us.

We have many fears—fear of the unknown, of our limitations, of failure, of pain, of growing old or of dying. Some people fear not being loved or being unloveable. All are sources of the constant worry that surfaces in our days.

It is important to recognize our fears, and not to ignore them. When we recognize them we can begin to deal with them. We can look our fears in the eye and know they do not control us. We do not need to give in to the worrying voices within us. The more we deal with our hidden fears the freer we will be to live in peace and to share our gifts.

After we recognize our fears, we must then see them in the light of God's love. Many people in scripture who met God or who were called on to do something with their gifts expressed their fear of doing so. They often protested their call because of these fears. They doubted that God could care that much for them, or they doubted their own ability to accept God's great love for them. Abraham feared the unknown land before him; Moses was scared that he would not say the right things; Samuel was afraid that Eli wouldn't believe him; Jacob awoke alarmed from his meeting with God; Zachary was overcome with fear when his prayer was heard; Mary feared the angel's greeting; the shepherds were alarmed when the glory of God shone around them; Joseph grew afraid of what God spoke to him in his dreams; Peter and his companions were frightened when their catch of fish was so great. Time and again the word of the Lord came to people who were fearful: "Do not be afraid. Have no fear. I am with you. I am your strength. I will support you. You have no need to be afraid."

God will not always take away our difficult situations because they are often a natural part of our earthly life, but we do know that this loving presence will always hold onto us, support us and strengthen us. We have this promise constantly in the scriptures. All we need to do is reach out in faith and trust. We will lessen our worry only if we believe more completely that God's fidelity and love will support and comfort us no matter what painful, difficult or fearful situations come to us.

We will learn how to deal with our fears if we allow ourselves to believe more totally in God's power working in us and through us. We have the example of Jesus to encourage us in this belief:

> You have known him not as a weakling, but as a power among you? Yes, but he was crucified through weakness, and still he lives now through the power of God. So then, we are weak, as he was, but we shall live with him, through the power of God . . . (2 Cor 13:3-4).

Jesus did not give in to his fears. He knew the Father was living in him, was doing the work, and that by himself he could do nothing (Jn 5:30; 14:10).

Because we are Christian our life story is also about the story of Jesus. When we recognize the events of our lives, both the happy and the difficult, we can gain a renewed vision and let go of some of the worrying. We will be better witnesses of that peace and we will be more open to hearing God's message.

This August I invite you to look into your life to see what worries you, what makes you afraid, what keeps you from mobilizing and using your giftedness and from sharing all that you are with others. When you find yourself feeling anxious or troubled or worried, pause to hear God saying to you, as was said so reassuringly and so often to the people of scripture, "Do not be afraid. I am with you."

May God bless our worrisome hearts and help them to be less fearful, more free, more peaceful this month.

For God himself has said: "I will not fail you or desert you, and so we can say with confidence: With the Lord to help me, I fear nothing . . ." (Heb 13:6).

Scripture Texts for Daily Prayer

Jn 6:16-21	Jesus said: "It is I. Do not be afraid."
Mt 1:18-22	"Joseph son of David, do not be afraid to take Mary home as your wife."
Mt 25:14-30	"I was afraid, and I went off and hid your talent in the ground."
Lk 12:4-12	"To you my friends I say: Do not be afraid. . . ."
Lk 24:36-43	The apostles were in a "state of alarm and fright." Jesus gives them his Spirit for courage and strength.
Lk 9:28-36	"The disciples were afraid. . . ."
1 Pt 3:13-17	"No one can hurt you if you are determined to do only what is right. . . . There is no need to be afraid or to worry about them. . . ."
Mt 14:22-33	". . . as soon as he (Peter) felt the force of the wind, he took fright and began to sink."
Lk 12:22-32	"I am telling you not to worry"
Mk 16:1-8	"The women came out and ran away from the tomb because they were frightened out of their wits; and they said nothing . . . for they were afraid."
1 Pt 5:5-11	"Unload all your worries on to him, since he is looking after you."
Phil 4:2-14	"There is no need to worry. . . ."
Mt 10:26-31	"Do not be afraid of those who kill the body but cannot kill the soul."

Jn 16:32-33	"In the world you will have trouble but be brave: I have conquered the world."
Is 50:4-10	"Let him trust in the name of Yahweh, let him lean on his God."
Wis 3:1-9	"Those who trust in him will understand the truth."
Ps 16	"I keep Yahweh before me always, for with him at my right hand nothing can shake me."
Ps 22	"In you our fathers put their trust, they trusted and you rescued them . . . they never trusted you in vain."
Ps 23	"Though I pass through a gloomy valley, I fear no harm."
Ps 37	"Be quiet before Yahweh, and wait patiently for him, not worrying. . . ."
Ps 62	"In God, I find shelter; rely on him people, at all times; unburden your hearts to him."
Ps 91	"My God in whom I trust."
Ps 118	"With Yahweh on my side, I fear nothing."
Gn 15:1-6	God said: "Have no fear, Abram, I am your shield; your reward will be very great."
Gn 28:10-22	Jacob meets the Lord God, wakes from his sleep and is fearful.
Is 41:9-14	"Do not be afraid, for I am with you; stop being anxious and watchful for I am your God."
Is 43:1-5	"Do not be afraid, for I have redeemed you."
1 Sm 3:1-19	"He (Samuel) was afraid to tell the vision to Eli. . . ."

Ex 3:1-6   "Moses covered his face, afraid to
                look at God."

Ps 27   "Yahweh is my light and my salva-
                tion, whom need I fear?"

Jesus came and stood among them. He said to them
"Peace be with you."   John 20:19

Jesus, you stand before me.
I feel it in my heart.
I sense you saying to me:

peace be with you,
        in your pressing days.
        amid your fragmentation.
        within your loneliness.
        with your concern of others.
        among those you care for.
        around your many questions.

peace, peace be with you,
for I am here. I am with you.
I offer you peace, my peace.
believe in me and my offer.

I will take you far beyond
all the fears, all the worries.
I will sink your spirit in calm,
in quiet, in truth, in me.

rest in me. rest in me.
peace be with you.

A Prayer for Inner Peace
and Transformation

Dear God, come with me into this day. Be with me where the dark things are. Take my hand through the valley of shadows; cast out fear and pride from my heart. Allow me to see that great hollow spot in me that has never been transformed into you. Take me to the "lazarus gulf"; do not spare me from the terror of it. Only, please God, do not let go of me for I will fall into my fear and leave you.

Praise be to you, shining shield of love. Alleluia to you, great God of warmth whose strong hand in my own keeps taking me to places I'd rather not go. My trust is in you, divine companion. O maker of mine, O giver of my life, trudge with me down my path of death into the murky mud of my sin. Stay with me as I see how unlike you I am, and then, beautiful gift of goodness, turn my heart around to face you. Allow me to behold the radiance of your astounding, wonderful beauty. Then, my loving God, I will be home.

Questions for Journal Keeping

Week 1   List your fears. What do you fear most? How many of your worries are based on your list of fears?

Week 2   Look at your list of fears carefully. Next to each one, write what each of these fears keeps you from being or doing. (How does that fear "paralyze" you?)

Week 3   Take several of your predominant fears and talk to God about them. Write your prayer to the one who can love all the fear out of you.

Week 4   Read the parable of Luke 12:22-32. Reflect on your specific worries and fears. Reflect on your experience of God's love and fidelity. Rewrite Luke 12 in your own words.

♣ SEPTEMBER

The Call to Discipleship

Jesus looked at him with love and told him, "There is one thing you lack. Go and sell everything you own and give the money to the poor, and you will then have treasure in heaven; then come, follow me."

Mark 10:21

"Invitation"

standing before me at the door
calling to me from the beach
gazing at me across the fields
walking toward me near the temple
turning to me on the mountain

over and over, my Lord,
you reach out to me
with the power of your heart
with the might of your love
with the force of your fidelity

what is it that you ask of me?
what is it that you offer to me?
to come? to follow? to belong?
to leave all? to let go? to be freed?

over and over, my Lord,
you invite me to yourself
you extend wholeness to me
you welcome me to your people

the invitation is there
I know it in my heart
I believe it in my being
I catch it in my prayer
I breathe it in my life

your welcome
your waiting
your very self is there
wanting me to come
desiring me to respond

O my Lord, I accept your invitation
O my Lord, I return the greeting
O my Lord, I want to see where you live
O my Lord, I will go where you will

O n one of my retreat days last summer, I stooped to pick up a fallen cottonwood leaf. My heart had been deep into reflection on discipleship and the leaf suddenly symbolized all that I had been praying. Very neatly eaten out of the leaf was a hole, thumbprint size. The tiny chomp marks of a caterpillar or some avaricious insect could easily be seen. My worn spirit looked long at that leaf. I said to myself, "I feel like that: eaten up by my work; the events of my calendar have taken a large space in me."

I have since asked myself many questions about ministry and the feeling that I sometimes get of being "eaten up." I have gone to God in prayer and questioned how much of myself I can afford to give and how much I need to keep. No easy answers have come but gradually I have learned some lessons about the "holes" I some-times feel in my spirit.

Morton Kelsey so wisely states in *Reaching for the Real:* "To one person hard work is only pain; to another it is an opportunity to create something of value." To this I'd add: "To some, hard work is just a chomped-out hole in one's spirit; to another, it is an opportunity to create something of value for the Kingdom of God." The secret to living with those empty places is to have the attitude of a disciple of Jesus.

I have never gotten used to the truth of discipleship: that to belong to Jesus means more than just a good feel-ing of being cherished and loved. I still struggle with the fact that there are conditions for discipleship and that "fol-lowing" means some hard demands and some constant conversion:

> Then Jesus said to his disciples, "If anyone wants to be a follower of mine, let him re-nounce himself and take up his cross and follow me. For anyone who wants to save his life will lose it; but anyone who loses his life for my sake will find it. What, then will a man gain if he wins the whole world and ruins his life? Or what has a man to offer in exchange for his life?" (Mt 16:24-26).

Too often I wish for a call free from obstacles, hurt, pain, disturbance, anxiety.

To follow Jesus in discipleship means that sometimes I will be rejected and misunderstood; I may not see results in ministry and I will need to give when nothing seems to be returned. "To follow" is to serve when the body and the spirit are weary and to never know what lies ahead. "To follow" is to live with mystery and to walk in faith, knowing that we are deeply loved. Even though discipleship is not always easy and even though sometimes we feel like there's a part of us that's been eaten out or chewed on, we can still live with a heart of peace and deep joy. The secret is that attitude which Kelsey spoke of: We know we are creating something of value because our hearts are set on the one who invites us to follow.

One of the disciples who recognized this and lived it out in his life was Paul. His life was truly a great love affair, a combination of loving and being loved by the Lord, of being willing to follow in the Lord's footsteps no matter what the cost. When Paul wrote to the Philippians, he penned a proclamation of a disciple's heart:

> I believe nothing can happen that will outweigh the supreme advantage of knowing Christ Jesus my Lord. For him I have accepted the loss of everything. . . . All I want is to know Christ and the power of his resurrection and to share his sufferings by reproducing the pattern of his death. . . . I am still running, trying to capture the prize for which Christ Jesus captured me (Phil 3:8,10,12).

Paul was willing to have some "chomping" on his life because his focus was always in discipleship with the one who had "captured him," the one who loved him so much. He knew what it was like to be called and cherished and to give his heart over to the God who invites and beckons. Paul did not rest in the good feeling, though. He kept the pattern of Jesus' death and resurrection close to mind and heart. That is why Paul could rejoice and celebrate life even when events seemed to create painful moments. Patterning of his own life on Jesus gave Paul energy and vision in his ministry. It was an opportunity for Paul "to create something of value."

To follow Jesus in discipleship, then, means that we, too, will be a people of great love. We too will lay down our lives for others. This is the price to be paid in discipleship—the giving away of our very selves. We will expect some emptying to go on in our lives, some "eating up" to take place. But it will not destroy us because we know that, like Jesus, we are about our Father's business. We can be sustained and strengthened by our love of God and our faith in his ever-abiding presence. We can have problems, frustrations, difficult situations and not allow them to embitter, disillusion or destroy us.

Even Jesus was weary from the journey: He sat down by the well of life, too tired to go on with his apostles, and he asked for refreshment. There were times when he had to withdraw to the hillsides, to be alone with the Father, to be refocused and re-energized in love. Jesus speaks to us out of his own life experience of ministry when he offers us these words of consolation: "Come to me, all who labor and are overburdened, and I will give you rest. Shoulder my yoke and learn from me, for I am gentle and humble in heart, and you will find rest for your souls. Yes, my yoke is easy and my burden light" (Mt 11:28-30).

Jesus knew it would take a lot of love and faith to remain in discipleship with him. He often turned to his disciples and reminded them of this in parables and in assurances of the Father's love for them. ("He told them a parable about the need to pray continually and never lose heart. . . . But when the Son of Man comes, will he find any faith on earth?"—Lk 18:1,8.) Jesus calmed the storms of his followers and he celebrated their friendships. He challenged them to greater freedom and to fidelity in servanthood. With all of this he continually reminded them to have faith. It is a challenge to all of us who give up too quickly, who lose sight of the kingdom, who rely mostly on ourselves and who complain bitterly when the "chomping" happens in our lives.

Because of the attitude of discipleship we can go to our tasks knowing that God dwells with us, strengthening and encouraging us. The yoke is easier and the burden lighter because it is for him that we are at work. It is his love that gives life to our ministry. It is our great desire to share this love that energizes our work. We follow Jesus and we, too, take care of ourselves by going to the quiet hillsides of our lives and renewing our love with the Father. In those moments apart from—as well as deep within—our ministry, we constantly draw strength and encouragement to give ourselves to others. It is a love that ebbs and flows from the Father's generosity. It moves through us to others. This is how Jesus came to his ministry and it is how we are meant to come to ours.

Thus, whatever our form of service, we know that we will be chomped on because we are disciples. ("A servant is not greater than his master"—Jn 15:20.) We know that this discipleship, this servanthood, does not have to destroy us. Rather, this very way of life can create new energy for the kingdom-in-process because we have kept our eyes fixed on the Lord and we know the joy of intimacy with him. We know that the mystery is "Christ among you, your hope of glory" and it is for this that we are willing to "struggle wearily on, helped by his power driving us irresistibly" (Col 1:27,29).

This month of September be especially aware of your feelings about your work, its ups and downs. Ask what causes those feelings. Notice how you let them influence your thinking and your actions. Look often at why you do your work and where your focus is.

Take time to reflect on your image of discipleship. What image would you choose to express your belief about discipleship—a chomped-out hole in a leaf, a cross, a heart, or some other significant object? Think about your image and picture it in your mind as you go to your prayer and to your work.

May you walk through your September days with the vision of "creating something of value" for the Kingdom of God.

Scripture Texts for Daily Prayer

Jn 1:35-51	The call of the disciples.
Jn 3:22-36	John the Baptist's testimony of discipleship: "He must grow greater, I must grow smaller."
Jn 6:22-31	"Jesus gave them this answer, 'This is working for God: you must believe in the one he has sent.' "
Jn 8:31-32	"If you make my word your home, you will indeed be my disciples."
Jn 12:20-36	"Unless a wheat grain falls on the ground and dies, it remains only a single grain."
Jn 13:1-16	"If I, then, the Lord and Master, have washed your feet, you should wash each other's feet."
Jn 14:1-21	"Whoever believes in me will perform the same works as I do myself."
Jn 15:1-17	"You did not choose me, no, I chose you; and I commissioned you to go out and bear fruit, fruit that will last."
Jn 15:18-27	"A servant is not greater than his master. If they persecuted me, they will persecute you, too."
Jn 17:1-11	". . . for I have given them the teaching you gave to me."
Jn 17:12-26	". . . so that the love with which you loved me may be in them, and so that I may be in them."
Mt 5:1-12	The core teaching for all disciples of Jesus.

Mt 5:13-16	"You are the light of the world. . . . Your light must shine in the sight of men. . . ."
Mt 7:21-29	The true disciple is the person "who does the will of my Father in heaven."
Mt 8:18-22	The hardships involved in discipleship.
Mt 10:17-25	"Do not worry about how to speak or what to say. . . ."
Mt 10:34-42	"Anyone who does not take his cross and follow in my footsteps is not worthy of me."
Mt 11:2-15	". . . And happy is the man who does not lose faith in me."
Mt 11:28-30	"Come to me, all you who labor and are overburdened and I will give you rest."
Mt 16:24-28	The condition of following Jesus.
Mt 18:1-4	"The one who makes himself as little as this little child is the greatest in the kingdom of heaven."
Mt 19:16-22	"Go and sell what you own and give the money to the poor, and you will have treasure in heaven; then come, follow me."
Mt 19:23-30	"Then Peter spoke. 'What about us?' he said to him. 'We have left everything and followed you. What are we to have, then?' "
Mt 20:20-28	"Can you drink the cup that I am going to drink?"
Eph 5:1-20	". . . and follow Christ by loving as he loved you."

Heb 10:32-39   "You will need endurance to do God's will and gain what he has promised."

Phil 3:7-16   "I believe nothing can happen that will outweigh the supreme advantage of knowing Christ Jesus my Lord."

a walk in morning stillness,
late September mist-in-air.
the pond so calm with quiet
that every golden-leafed tree
looks deeply back at me.

> I think the passage about Abraham,
> I pray the passage about Abraham.
> the quiet, the pond, possess me.
> the reality of following my God
> seeps through every silent moment.

then in the corner of my eye,
a treasure and a gift for the day:
the geese sail through the quiet grey sky,
not a sound from their autumn voices,
only the whisper of strong wings wending.

> Abraham. geese. following.
> he let his God lead him.
> the geese follow their hearts,
> give themselves in faithful journey.

the questions in my life this day
are walking away with treasured answers:
come, follow me. follow me. follow me.
strong wings will bear the journey,
faithful hearts will hear the music.
come, follow me. follow me. follow me.

Prayer of a Disciple

Loving God, that you would think my heart capable of belonging to you! You have filled my life with your goodness in so many ways. I hear the call to give myself to your love in an ever deeper and more complete way. I long to follow you so totally that you are evident in every fiber of my life.

I pray for faith, that long-lasting, true sense of you that weathers all storms, that comes across the waters bravely when you ask for me, that sinks into your love and lets go of anxieties and worries, that looks long into the eyes of others' sufferings, that takes care to be gentle with sinners and those whose lives are never free from intense pain of body or spirit.

I pray for love, that great and generous-enough love that looks compassionately upon all, that love which accepts others with their mystery, doubt, hesitation, that love which reaches out even though there is no response in return, that love which is patient and kind, that kind of love, which is your love, never jealous, boastful or conceited, that love which is never rude or selfish but rather, always ready to excuse, to trust, to hope and to endure whatever comes.

I yearn for you to be the intimate Master, the one at whose feet I can sit and ponder the message, the one whose hand I can hold and walk with when I am afraid, the one at whose side I can sit as we taste the meal, the one whose robe I can touch, even in the crowd.

I will follow. I will rejoice in loving you and being loved by you. I need to hear your voice over and over and over again. I need to keep reclaiming all the intimacy you hold out to me. I need to let go of all the selfishness that binds me. I need to believe that you want to win over my heart completely.

O Jesus, master, shepherd, lover, leader! Here I am again. Please claim me as your own.

Questions for Journal Keeping

Week 1 "They left everything and followed him" (Lk 5:11). What does it mean to you to follow Jesus? How have you experienced this "following" in your life? (Recall significant moments in your life when you felt a call to follow Jesus.)

Week 2 Name and identify characteristics and aspects of your personality and of your life experiences that are helps to you in following the master.

Week 3 What do you find most difficult in discipleship? What riches does Jesus ask you to leave behind in order to follow him more wholeheartedly?

Week 4 Imagine yourself to be at the place where Jesus calls his disciples to "follow." See Jesus looking on you with love. What does he say to you? What is your response?

The Vulnerable Autumn Leaves

Autumn,
the season of vulnerability,
when the great arms of oak
stretch their summer leaves
to the wild October winds.

all that has been life and green
is stripped from strong trees,
and the tall, wide branches
seem to be deathly wounded.

across the lawns in layers
lie the near-dead leaves;
onto the forest floors they fall
as if to say: "all is lost."

this is the season of vulnerability
when trees open wide to wounding,
when all the summer security
is given away to another season.

wiser are the trees than humans
who clutch small arms round self,
shielding their fragile hearts
and stifling future springtimes.

I finally realize why I've grown to appreciate autumn so much. It is because the trees tell me so much about life, especially about the inner seasons of our lives. Each year as I begin to notice that the leaves are going golden, I reflect that the trees seem to give themselves over to the "letting go" process much more freely than humans. Trees readily allow autumn to have their summer leaves. Trees allow the frost to touch them and the wind to toss them. They allow the season to make it appear that all is lost and that there is no green growth left. But they know better, for even at their most barren moment, when one can look among the branches and see scars and knotholes the leaves once hid, the trees already show terminal buds with the secret of next spring's leafing in them.

We humans have a lot to learn from autumn trees. No one of us wants to be so surrendered, so vulnerable to winter as the October trees. Yet, each of us, if we are truly open to growth and change, will experience this in our inner selves. Our relationships and our experiences of life will ask us to be open, to be willing to let go in order that new growth can come.

New growth means change. Trees tell us this. Life tells us this. Jesus tells us this. One of the most beautiful aspects of the Incarnation is that the Son of God allowed himself to be vulnerable. He came as one of us and he opened himself up in love to the possibility of failure, being wounded, misunderstood, and rejected, all of those things that we know as "daily dyings," like those autumn leaves fast falling from trees.

Every time Jesus opened himself to others, every time he reached out or spoke up, every time he touched or received from others, he allowed himself to be vulnerable. Because of this vulnerability people said:

"How can this man talk like that? He is blaspheming. Who can forgive sins but God?" (Mk 2:7)

"Why does he eat with tax collectors and sinners?" (Mk 2:16)

"Where did this man get all this? What is this wisdom that has been granted him?" (Mk 6:2)

"Why do your disciples not respect the tradition of the elders?" (Mk 7:5)

"What authority have you for acting like this?" (Mk 11:28)

Jesus continued to be vulnerable even to death on the cross because he knew that his life was a blessing to others. He grew ever more deeply in love with the Father, drawing strength and trust and courage from that relationship. It was his deep vulnerability that encouraged Jesus to pray:"Let your will be done, not mine" (Lk 22:43) and "Into your hands I commit my spirit" (Lk 23:46). It was this surrender that led to death and then to the tremendous new growth of resurrection. It is the faith-moment that has given courage for change to all autumn hearts ever since.

C. S. Lewis understands well this vulnerability of Jesus when he writes: "To love at all is to be vulnerable." Lewis cautions that the only way of being sure we will not be hurt or wounded is to give our heart to no one and never to be vulnerable. If we do this, then we lock our heart up in a tomb of selfishness where it will eventually become "unbreakable, impenetrable, irredeemable." He encourages us to look to Jesus and to draw near to God, "not by trying to avoid the sufferings inherent in all loves, but by accepting them and offering them to Him; throwing away all defensive armor" (C. S. Lewis, *The Four Loves*).

Jesus referred to throwing away all defensive armor when he said, "Only if you lose your life for my sake will you find it." Jesus was talking about the autumns in our lives—those moments of vulnerability when we are asked to shed our armor, to risk relationships, when we open ourselves to try something new so that more of our giftedness can be shared, when we walk the extra mile or turn the other cheek or forgive seventy times seven.

Being vulnerable does not mean being weak and allowing anyone or anything to hurt us. It is actually a great inner strength which comes from freely choosing to be open to being wounded because we are open to loving in the manner in which Jesus loved. To be vulnerable in this way is to *freely choose*:

—to be open to the other, no matter who that other is

—to stand firmly on our convictions amid controversy

—to risk our voice or actions even though there's a possibility of being misunderstood, rejected, thwarted or even condemned.

—to share from our faith even though we may be questioned or ignored, laughed at or thought to be stupid

—to risk failure in order to discover and use our giftedness and potential

—to love and to continue loving even when there is no positive response from the one being loved

Most importantly, to be vulnerable is to know the paradoxical power in surrendering ourselves to God. It is to allow the power of God's spirit to take over and to move through our being. It is to know that by ourselves we can do nothing, but with a surrendered heart we can do all things through the one who gives us strength. With a surrendered heart, we can have the power in us to do infinitely more than we can ask or imagine. We can easily forget this gift of power and try to shield ourselves from any possible hurt, pain, question, doubt, heartache, risk, any of the tough stuff of life.

Again, I think of the trees and I look to them. Have you ever noticed that some trees still have leaves hanging onto them in deep December? Long after autumn the dead brown things clutch in clumps at ends of branches or trail alone at the end of a twig. They must know that eventually winter claims them all. Like the leaves are those humans who think that growth is possible without letting go. They deny, fight, or refuse to accept what is being asked in order that new life can take place.

This October, let us pause and allow the falling leaves to remind us of the call to be vulnerable, the call to be open to the possibility of being hurt, the call to accept and to grow from the daily dyings of our days and to love as Jesus loved.

Go for a walk in the forest or just down the street if you have some trees nearby whose leaves have turned. Let your heart roam through the leaves. Think thoughts of vulnerability. Pick up a leaf. Take it home with you. Place it somewhere where you will see it often. Let it remind you of the call to be vulnerable.

Take time to browse through a gospel. Note all the times that Jesus opened himself to hurt and misunderstanding. Allow yourself to be a bit more open and vulnerable to someone whom you love. Surrender yourself a bit more to God's power working through you. Let October be a time when the value of vulnerability is strengthened in your life.

Scripture Texts for Daily Prayer

The vulnerability of Jesus . . .

Lk 4:1-13	in the desert.
Lk 5:17-26	as he forgave sins.
Mk 3:1-6	as he reached out to others.
Mk 6:1-6	in his hometown teaching.
Mk 7:1-23	in not being understood.
Mk 2:13-16	as he ate with outcasts.
Jn 19:1-7	as he faced Pilate.
Lk 22:39-46	in his agony.
Lk 22:47-53	with Judas.

The vulnerability of gospel people

Acts 7:55-60	Stephen.
Acts 9:1-19	Saul (Paul).
Lk 7:36-50	The woman who anointed Jesus' feet.
Jn 21:15-19	Peter.
Lk 8:40-48	The woman with a hemorrhage.
Jn 4:1-42	The woman at the well.
Lk 15:11-32	The prodigal—coming home.
Jn 19:25-27	The Mother of Jesus.
Mk 1:40-45	A leper.
Mk 10:46-52	Bartimaeus.
Mk 7:24-30	The Syrophoenician woman.
Mk 6:17-29	John the Baptist.
Lk 7:1-10	The centurion.
Jn 5:1-18	A sick man at the Pool of Bethzatha.
Jn 8:1-11	The adulterous woman.

The vulnerability of some Old Testament people

1 Sm 1:9-20	Hannah.
Ex 3:1-6	Moses before Yahweh.
Jer 1:4-10	Jeremiah in his call.
Gn 22:1-19	Abraham in his surrender.
Gn 42:1-24	Joseph with his brothers.
Ru 1:1-22	Ruth in her fidelity.

something unnamed
is being called forth
in the depths

>   it has the familiar sound
>   of an Abraham
>   and the quiet certainty
>   of a sunrise

it has the movement
of geese surging
past a season

>   of trees surrendering
>   to another snowfall
>   or another leafing

something unnamed
keeps calling
>   beckoning
>   rooting
>   growing

something unnamed
asks for surrender
>   vulnerability
>   given-over-ness
>   abandonment
>   powerlessness

ah yes
the truth takes time
to be named

and even more time
to be accepted

Prayer

Dear God of Autumn, I see how the trees have suddenly changed. There are so many hues of dying in the colored leaves. As always I cry out inside: "Not yet! Please, not yet!" Why is this cry so strong? Why does it never leave me? Every year I think that I have finally accepted summer's going but every year I fight the loss of warmth and green. Is it my humanness and my intense grasp on life? Is it a lack of maturity in my own spirituality? Am I still so far away from accepting the truth of the Paschal mystery? I wonder about that. No answers come to me. Only the questions that I know so well. In the meantime, the air keeps on getting cooler and frost threatens to wrap itself around pumpkins.

Jesus, master of the seasons of the heart, take this dread of winter in me and transform it into joy and trust. Help me to know that every season has its own reason to exist and that each season brings its own set of blessings. Grant me the grace of vulnerability so that I can surrender my heart to you and love as you loved. Walk with me when I want to run away from the negatives of life instead of desiring to grow through them. Amen.

Questions for Journal Keeping

Week 1 Reflect on the moments of your life when you were vulnerable. Choose one that is especially significant. What happened? How did you feel? What did you think? Was there growth in this experience? What does it tell you about your life?

Week 2 Hold your heart alongside the heart of Jesus. List the qualities of his loving. How vulnerable are you in the light of these qualities?

Week 3 C. S. Lewis: "To love at all is to be vulnerable." Recall the significant loves of your life. What have you learned from your experience of loving?

Week 4 What were the opportunities in your life this month which called you to greater vulnerability and risk-taking?

The Gifts of Life, Love and Time

"There is more happiness in giving than in receiving."
Acts 20:35

Jesus
every once in a while
I realize how absurd
your conditions for following:

that feeling of being town pump
for some of those who come
only when they're in need of water.

they come expecting to draw
from the heart of a well
long time facing its dryness.

they come for life and newness
thinking as they do
that wells which offer water
will never go dry.

and in some ways it's true,
for just when I've tasted dust
there you are
with another gush of goodness.

still, Lord,
every once in a while
I find it hard to stand
silent, emptied, bone-dry,
knowing it's one of those
crazy conditions
you put on those who follow.

Novamber: Thanksgiving Day, harvest times, awareness of blessings, gratitude for gifts. It is significant and necessary for us to ponder deeply all that we have been given. If we reflect quietly and honestly, we can be almost overwhelmed by all that is ours. God has been very generous. None of the gifts has been earned. God gives all gifts freely. Even Jesus is an abundant, free gift to us. God is lavish in love, generous in the outpouring of goodness. This great generosity can draw us to look at our own generosity: How generous have we been with others in our lives? Are we people who freely give of our treasures? Do we yearn to have the heart of our God, the one who lavishes love upon us freely? Do we cherish deeply all that we are and all that we have been given? Do we hold that love with open hands, allowing it to be readily available to others or do we clutch it to ourselves in fear that we might lose it?

I've noticed something happening in our world at an ever more intense level. It scares me. Many people experience economic problems that do not seem to go away. Yet others have begun to clutch things to themselves. It seems so easy to allow a quiet greed to smother the generosity of our hearts. People seem afraid that they will not have enough.

But how much is enough? Do we need all the collections, electrical gadgets, the extra snacks and other things that we have come to use regularly? What is enough? We seem to feel that we just do not have enough. We are busy shopping, buying, searching for bargains and sales. What is the difference between having what we need and having what we want? What is the point at which a person becomes generous?

This feeling of not having enough stretches over into other dimensions of our existence. When we clutch material things to our hearts, we also begin to cling to things of the spirit. Life, love and time are three of our greatest gifts. Yet, it is so easy to be stingy and clutch them to ourselves. The more time we spend on the material aspects of our lives the less life, love and time we will have to share with others. And so, we begin to say: "I'm sorry I haven't been to see you; I've just not had the time." Or, "I can't help out with that. My calendar's much too full." We must always balance giving and receiving. Yet, if our scheduling and our decisions mainly center on ourselves and, if we rarely have time for others, perhaps we are hanging on too tightly to our own blessings. Perhaps we have become scared that there won't be enough life, love and time left for us.

A generous heart freely gives and can live without some of the material things we think are so desperately needed. A generous heart is also one that can give freely of the greater, nonmaterial gifts such as compassion, understanding, patience and forgiveness.

Giving freely means that we give with no strings attached, that we give without counting the cost. How many times have we heard ourselves or others say, "I'm not sending them a card. They didn't send us one last year." Or, "I'm not going to give him a present. He never acknowledged the other one I gave him." Or, "I'm not going to help with that volunteer project. No one ever appreciates all the hours that go into it."Or, "Have they ever done anything for us?"

In being generous we do need to take care of ourselves and to give ourselves the gifts of life, love and time. Yet, there is such a fine line between being self-centered and in being self-loving and caring well for self. I have often struggled with this tension. I see it often in the lines of my journals. Not so long ago I wrote:

> Yesterday, the geese and ducks at the pond gathered around my feet as I fed them. They were so excited and pressed in closely, flying, quacking, honking, and begging to be fed. Somehow the story of Jesus and bread seemed so much more real as I reached out with the crumbs to those begging creatures. I thought of how often I feel "eaten up" by others, constantly being called on to give and to share what I have and who I am, and how I miss the beauty of being able to be food, to be the nour-

ishment for them. The Christ in me will always be food for others, even when I think the cupboard of my heart is bare. He will sustain me and renew my weary, empty heart with new life and giftedness.

In the midst of this struggle between generosity and self-centeredness, I have come to believe with all my heart that we need not fear to be generous. If our priorities regarding life, love and time are centered on the gospel, our needs will be met. Anne Frank once wrote "No one has ever become poor by giving." God does provide. Generosity encourages us to rely on God. I have learned this through my own experiences of giving and receiving.

One Christmas I decided to give away some of my treasures, items I had hung onto and valued because of the givers. As I slowly gave these gifts away, I noticed that almost every one of them returned to me in some form: A candle or plant or poster would soon be back in another color or shape. One day I gave a not-yet-worn sweater to some people whose home had been destroyed by fire. The next day a belated Christmas gift arrived at my door. Yes, a sweater! Many times since I have experienced similar "miracles" of giving and receiving. They continue to convince me that "no one ever becomes poor by giving."

This has also been true of gifts of the heart. I recall once when I was pressed for time but I took the half hour for prayer anyhow. When I returned from the Eucharist my phone was ringing. Someone was calling me to tell me that the workshop for the evening had been cancelled. I was suddenly given a whole evening in return for my half hour of time shared with the Lord. This happens over and over with human friendship, too. I offer it and find it is returned a hundredfold; I give compassion and receive it in abundance at those moments when I am most in need.

These experiences of giving and receiving have helped me believe more firmly in generosity and have deepened my desire to be more openhanded. Still, I continue to struggle with my selfishness. My heart still clutches and hangs on at times. I occasionally regret and begrudge my giving of time, and hesitate before sharing a thing I value, like a good book that might not be returned. I believe in generosity and I believe that our hearts are meant to be like those of our generous God, the one who lavishes us with so many good gifts.

November is a good time to remember and to thank this generous God. It also seems to be an appropriate season to reflect on our gifts and the call to share them gratefully.

Take time each day to pray the prayer of "open hands." Just be in prayer with your hands open, palms up. Let the attitude of your heart be one in which you freely place in your open hands all the gifts you've been given by God, knowing that you can give away any of these gifts and trusting that God will provide what you need.

Take time to reflect on the people of your life who are special gifts to you; choose one who might need to hear your appreciation and affirmation. Write that person a letter of thanksgiving.

Give away something material that you cherish and hold dear. Give it away with no strings attached.

Give away something nonmaterial that you cherish and hold dear. Give it away with no strings attached.

As you reflect on all the ways that God has been generous to you and as you give away some of what you cherish and hold dear, may your heart grow in the wisdom that "no one ever becomes poor by giving."

Scripture Texts for Daily Prayer

1 Tm 6:17-19   "Warn those who are rich in this world's goods . . . not to set their hopes on money . . . but on God. . . ."

2 Cor 6:3-10   ". . . for people having nothing though we have everything."

1 Thes 3:6-13	"May the Lord be generous in increasing your love and make you love one another. . . ."
1 Jn 3:1-2	"Think of the love that the Father has lavished on us. . . ."
1 Cor 16:13-24	"I want you in your turn to put yourselves at the service of people like this. . . ."
2 Pt 1:3-11	"He (God) has given us all the things that we need for life and for true devotion. . . ."
1 Cor 13:1-13	"If I give away all that I possess . . . but am without love, it will do me no good."
Rom 12:9-21	"Make real friends with the poor."
Acts 20:28-38	". . . remembering the words of the Lord Jesus, who himself said, 'There is more happiness in giving than in receiving.' "
Sir 18:15-18	"A word is better than a good present, but a generous man is ready with both."
1 Cor 1:1-9	"You have been enriched in so many ways."
Sir 29:8-13	"Deposit generosity in your storerooms and it will release you from every misfortune."
Lk 6:20-26	"How happy are you who are poor: yours is the kingdom of God. . . . Alas, for you who have your fill now: you shall go hungry."
Ps 112	"Quick to be generous, he gives to the poor, . . . men such as this will always be honored."
Mt 6:19-21	"Do not store up treasures for yourselves on earth."

Sir 4:31-5:8	"Do not let your hands be out-stretched to receive, yet closed when the time comes to give back."
Sir 7:32-36	"Be generous in your gifts to all the living."
Eph 2:1-10	"But God loved us with so much love that he was generous in his mercy."
2 Cor 9:10-15	". . . and made richer in every way, you will be able to do all the generous things which, through us, are the cause of thanksgiving to God."
Prv 3:1-10	"Honor Yahweh with what goods you have and with the first fruits of all your returns."
Prv 3:27-35	"Do not refuse a kindness to anyone who begs it, if it is in your power to perform it."
Prv 11:24-28	"The generous soul will prosper . . . ."
Prv 28:20-28	"He who gives to the poor shall never want. . . ."
2 Cor 8: 9-15	"Remember how generous the Lord Jesus was. . . ."
2 Cor 9:6-9	"God loves a cheerful giver."
Mt 5:38-46	"If you love those who love you, what right have you to claim any credit?"
Dt 15:7-11	"When you give . . . you must give with an open heart."
Lk 6:36-38	"The amount you measure out is the amount you will be given back."
Lk 12:13-21	"Be on your guard against avarice of any kind."
Lk 21:1-4	"But she from the little she had has put in all she had to live on."

the widow of Zarephath
1 Kings 17:10-16

a woman to be admired,
a woman truly poor in spirit,
she did not refuse the prophet
the "little water" for him to drink;
she did not refuse to share
the tiny bit of bread she had saved.

and God provided.

she never went hungry; she never went thirsty;
of her emptiness she gave
and God provided the fullness.

humility, trust, faith;
me?
I'd probably say:
get your own drink,
who do you think you are?
go away. I don't even have enough
to get myself through another day.

the widow: unselfish.
myself: so selfish, still.
how many bedraggled prophets
come daily to the doorstep
of my empty, naked heart?
and I refuse to feed them
because I am so poor.

Prayer—
A Litany of Generosity

(Response to each: Gracious God, give us generous hearts.)

—to share whatever gift it is that you have given to us . . .

—to acknowledge you as the giver of all good gifts . . .

—to give without counting the cost . . .

—to share without expecting something in return . . .

—to be wise in the way of caring for ourselves and others . . .

—to hold all of our treasures and values with open hands . . .

—to have gospel priorities and to align our life, love and time in their light . . .

—to be gracious and unbegrudging in our giving. . .

—to recognize the abundance of blessings in each passing day . . .

—to know the freedom that comes with true generosity . . .

—to experience the heart of the widow giving her mite . . .

—to accept our talents, whether many or few, and to use them in service of the Kingdom . . .

—to grow in giving thanks for everything . . .

—to be happy with having what we need and to be wise enough to know what it is that we want and do not need . . .

—to fall more deeply in love with the God of all
generosity so that our hearts are strong enough
to give away freely whatever is asked . . .

O gracious God, who so generously lavishes our lives
with goodness, create in our hearts a deep center of gratitude, a center that grows so strong in its thanksgiving that
sharing freely of our treasures becomes the norm and the
pattern of our existence. Remind us often of how much
you cherish us, of how abundantly you have offered gifts
to us, especially in the hours of our greatest need. May
we always be grateful for your reaching into our lives with
surprises of joy, growth, and unearned love. Amen.

Questions for Journal Keeping

Week 1   In what ways has God been generous to you, especially the past year?

Week 2   Take some prayer time to reflect on all the gifts you have in your life. Make a list of all these gifts. Are there people, things, intangibles in your life to which you cling and which you do not hold freely in open hands? Which ones are you unwilling to share?

Week 3   What were some of your predominant feelings the past week? Were any of these related to the call to be generous?

Week 4   Write your prayer of thanksgiving to our generous God.

♣ DECEMBER

A Welcoming Nest

That Christ may live in your hearts through faith.
Ephesians 3:17

looking high into winter trees
I see the distant nests
cradled in arms of branches.

nests: round, full of warmth,
softness in the welcoming center,
a circle of earth's tiny goodness,
flown from the far corners,
patiently pieced together,
and hollowed into a home.

nests: awaiting the treasure of life,
simple, delicate dwelling places
from which song will eventually echo
and freedom of wings give flight.

advent has been on my mind.

prepare the nest of heart.
patch up the broken parts.
place more softness in the center.
sit and warm the home with prayer.
give the Christ a dwelling place.

If you look high into the trees on December days can see little bunches of nests everywhere. They remind me of Advent. Instead of getting a nest ready that will be round and welcoming for an egg and the future young life, I am getting a Christ-home ready within my life. I am trying to prepare a dwelling place for the Lord, a warm, well-hollowed, hospitable place where the life of my God will deepen and mature in me.

A nest is a home prepared from everyday fragments: twigs, dry grasses, pebbles, mud, saliva, feathers, and many other little bits of very ordinary things. Hummingbirds use moss and spider webs to make their nests while thrushes make a clay foundation and line the interior with a mixture of decayed wood and cow dung.

Whatever the kind of nest, or wherever they are placed, they are hollowed as a dwelling place to receive the gift of life.

Each Advent for many years now, I have read and prayed Caryll Houselander's *Reed of God*. She writes beautifully of the nest as a symbol, and it speaks to my heart of how the word of God "was made flesh and dwelt among us." She writes of how we are receivers of that word as nests are receivers of new life. Houselander refers to Mary as the "warm nest" who received Jesus into her life and nurtured him. She asks about us being warm nests: "Does he (Jesus) ask to be fostered, swaddled, cherished, the little unfledged bird in the human heart?" What does the presence of God in our life mean to us? What is it for the word to have dwelt among us? How does that word continue to dwell among us?

I believe that the word comes ever so quietly and in ever so ordinary a way. The twigs of our trials and tensions, the soft down of our love and fidelity, the pebbles of our patience and pain, the straw of our struggles and strivings, the mud of our humanness and growing, the dry grass of our surrender and our daily dyings. These are the content of our nests where God asks us to hollow out a welcoming place. Jesus comes to us in the midst of everyday fragments and asks us to create space for him where he has never been before, or places where he is no longer welcome. All the bits and pieces of our lives, like those bits and pieces that form birds' nests, are where he awaits a birthing. All of us are meant to know and to deeply appreciate the joy and privilege of this nesting, of this homing of the God who waits for us to openly receive the life offered to us.

Advent, then, might be called a season of nesting. Human hearts are asked to prepare a way for the Lord. Just as Christmas celebrates the coming of Emmanuel so many years ago and how he continues to come and dwell among us, so Advent is the time to prepare each year for the coming of God-with-us. Emmanuel comes, filling the nests of our hearts repeatedly with a special presence that we sense and know, a presence which we can quickly disregard because of the inner traffic and noise of our daily activity.

Advent beckons to us. Be still. Be alert. Get into the spirit of the Old Testament folks and yearn for the Savior. Cry out to God. Cry out to be open and receptive. Sharpen your awareness of the God who dwells within. Open up. Hollow out. Receive. Welcome the one who comes.

When John writes of Jesus saying: "Make your home in me, as I make mine in you" he could well have written: "Make your nest in me as I make my nest in you." If we reflect on this truth of the indwelling God we would be astounded and overwhelmed. We would find it so easy to yearn for more, to cry out in welcome. We would run and invite everyone to our nest, to come and see how we have been blessed beyond our expectations. This gift keeps entering our lives. That is why it is so important to reflect during Advent, to ponder the redemption, to not let the hurried pace of Christmas take us from our nesting time. We need to hold the mystery and the wonder of the Incarnation near to our hearts in solitude and in prayer.

This Advent I invite you to prepare a dwelling place for the Christ in your life. Prepare your heart daily. Develop a deeper awareness of how he dwells among us. Each morning pray a simple prayer of "Come Lord Jesus, dwell with me this day"; each evening take a few minutes to think about the nest you are preparing for the Lord; reflect on how God has been in your life and how you've been open to his dwelling. You might look at the trees more often, even take a special walk to do so. (Walk slowly. Stop to look at the nests. Ponder the message that is there for you.) You could also make an artificial nest from little bits of things around your house or office. Hang the nest on one of the branches of your Christmas tree or place it in the center of your advent wreath to remind you to prepare a home in your heart for Jesus. You might write a prayer and place it in the nest you've created.

One of the significant ways that God dwells in our midst is through the people around us. This December, when we are busily preparing for so many things, ask ourselves: "Lord, when did I bake cookies or bread for you? When did I get a Christmas tree for you? When did I welcome you at work or in the restaurant or in the grocery store? When did I shop for you or write you a long letter? When did I receive a card or a letter from you? When did I take the time to go and to visit you?" And if we have been open and receptive to the word, if we have warmed the nest within us, we will hear the word say to us: "Whenever you welcomed these, you welcomed me"

Keep welcoming Emmanuel into your heart-nest this Advent season, remembering that it is there that Jesus continues to be born and desires to make a home, if only we will receive him and warm the nest with love.

Scripture Texts for Daily Prayer

God is at home in our hearts:

Rom 8:1-11 "If Christ is in you then your spirit is life itself."

Jn 15:1-7 "Make your home in me, as I make mine in you."

Jn 14:22-31 "We shall come to him and make our home with him."

Eph 3:14-21 "So that Christ may live in your hearts through faith."

1 Cor 3:5-17 "Didn't you realize that you were God's temple and that the Spirit of God was living among you?"

2 Cor 1:12-22 "The Spirit, that we carry in our hearts. . . ."

2 Cor 4:6-12 "We are only the earthenware jars that hold this treasure. . . ."

2 Cor 13:5-10 "Do you acknowledge that Jesus Christ is really in you?"

Phil 4:1-9 "The Lord is very near. There is no need to worry."

Col 1:24-29 "The mystery is Christ among you."

Col 3:1-4 "The life you have is hidden with Christ in God."

Col 3:5-27 "There is only Christ: he is everything and he is in everything."

1 Jn 4:7-16 ". . . as long as we love one another God will live in us."

Rev 21:1-4 "Here God lives among men. He will make his home among them. . . ."

God dwells among the people:

Lv 26:3-13 "I will set up my dwelling among you."

Ex 13:21-22	The nearness of God to the Israelites.
Ex 33:18-23	"Yahweh said: 'Here is a place beside me.' "
Dt 1:29-33	"Yahweh carried you, as a man carries his child, all along the road you travelled on the way to this place."
Dt 4:1-8	"And indeed, what great nation is there that has its gods so near as Yahweh our God is to us whenever we call to him?"
Is 41:10-14	"For I, Yahweh, your God, I am holding you by the right hand."

Hospitality of the Heart/Welcoming the Christ:

Rom 12:9-13	"Make hospitality your special care."
Mt 1:18-25	"He (Joseph) took his wife to his home."
Lk 1:26-38	Mary welcomes the Word into her life.
Lk 1:39-45	Mary and Elizabeth welcome one another.
Lk 2:1-20	The newly born Savior is welcomed by angels and shepherds.
Lk 2:36-38	Anna welcomes the Christ into her life.
1 Pt 4:7-11	"Welcome each other into your houses without grumbling."
Heb 13:1-6	"Remember always to welcome strangers."
Heb 10:19-25	"Let us be concerned for each other."
Lk 10:38-42	"Martha welcomed him."

She wrapped him in swaddling clothes and laid him in a
manger because there was no room for them in the inn.

Luke 2:7

no room for you in the city, Jesus.
so many doors were tried and closed to you.
so many places did not warm you with welcome.

there is still a coming.
there is still a Bethlehem.
it is the city of my heart
with no room to give you welcome.

it is the manger of my inner self
where your request is made,
searching for an entrance
to my poor and empty dwelling.

Advent is a time for waiting.
I will wait faithfully
for slow recognition
of the closed doors in my Bethlehem.

Advent is a time of yearning.
I will keep on longing for you.
I will try to do so patiently.

Advent is a time of hoping.
I will seek the strong stirring sureness
that it is possible to open doors.

Advent is a time of coming.
I will pray with all the church:
come. come. come, Lord Jesus.
welcome into my home of love.

And Lord, when it is time to say:
this is the Christmas day,
I pray that you will warmly be welcome
in the Bethlehem of my heart,
giving birth in my newly opened places.

A Christmas Prayer for Loved Ones

For those who have an abundance of love, a bounty in heart and home, keep them mindful of the world's poor, lift their voices often to you in gratitude, loving God.

For those who carry hurts and angers and other heartaches, help them to feel the peace which only you can give and the grace to let go of long burdening memories.

For those who struggle with the lack of this world's riches, those who know what unemployment and empty pockets feel like, gift them with a counting of blessings which are often hidden and far more valuable than earthly treasure.

For those whose faith has grown dim and whose sense of you seems far away, raise in their hearts a great yearning for you that will not cease and a desire for the truth that cannot be ignored.

For those who are tired, weary, worn from a constant generous giving of their lives in love, be their energy and enthusiasm, be a great and deep spark of light and happiness within them.

For those who grieve the goodbye of a loved one and whose hearts are very lonely this time of year, touch them with dear memories and transform the inner missing and heartache into a vision of what lies far beyond this time and space.

For those whose lives speak of growing old, bless again and again with peace and serenity, let them know what gentle witnesses they are to all of us who still ponder the meaning of life and growth.

And finally, savior God, for those with young eyes, keep their hearts full of wonder, and thank you for slipping some of their delight and simplicity into our own hearts each time we celebrate the Christmas moment. Amen.

Questions for Journal Keeping

Week 1 How is the "nest" of your heart in relation to the dwelling of the Lord? Do you have room for your God? Is there an awareness in your life of the presence of the Lord? Where, in your life, does the Christ most seek a welcome?

Week 2 What about the hospitality of your heart in relation to the people around you? Are there people who come to your door and are refused entrance? How welcoming are you when you are busy and pressed? What needs to happen in your life to enable you to be more open and receptive, more hospitable?

Week 3 The time of the savior's birth is near. What is yearning in you this week? What are the places in your life that cry out for redemption? Name these. Pray/write your prayer of yearning.

Week 4 Are there people and events in your life this Advent season that have encouraged you and deepened your hope?

A Prayer for Hospitality
to the Mother of Jesus

Mary, the quality of your visit to Elizabeth draws me to prayer. You teach me so much about welcoming others and of being other-centered. You hurried quickly to where the need was. You thought of Elizabeth. You gave her joy, hope and promise, or rather, you allowed the Lord to do all of that through you. You believed in the promise made to you by your God. Is that why you could give and share, and visit the way you did? You touched Elizabeth's spirit and she felt the goodness of God in her life. Mary, you understood so well God's great love for you. You trusted him so totally. Your welcoming presence met Elizabeth and she cried out in recognition of the fulness of God within you.

Mary, dear woman of God pray for us, that we can be spiritual people of quality, of promise, of welcoming presence. Help us to be full of hospitality, welcoming the Christ in all and allowing the Christ within us to be met and visited. Amen.